FROM BONDAGE TO BOLDNESS

A Journey from Abuse and Fear to God's Power

ROSE HOWARD

Print ISBN: 978-1-63616-248-5

Published By Opportune Independent Publishing Co.

Printed in the United States of America

For permission requests, please email the publisher with the subject line as" Attention: Permissions Coordinator"
to the email address below:
Info@Opportunepublishing. com

PROLOGUE

Fear. It has a way of seeping into the deepest corners of your life, often without you realizing it. For years, fear was my companion, my guide, and my captor. It whispered in my ear, telling me I wasn't enough, that leaving would mean losing my family and possibly my life and that my life was destined to remain in chains. Fear wrapped itself around my decisions, dictating my every move. It became the lens through which I saw the world, blinding me to the possibilities of freedom, hope, and peace.

This is not just a story about the abuse I endured—though the abuse was real and devastating. It's about the battle for my soul, for my identity, and for my faith. It's about how I allowed fear to rule my life for so long, and how I finally found the courage to confront it. Through the grace of God, I began to see fear for what it truly is—a lie. A lie that only holds power if we let it.

For years, I lived in darkness, bound by fear, anger, and shame. I prayed, but my prayers were hollow because I hadn't yet learned to truly surrender. I wanted freedom, but I didn't know how to step into it. I wanted peace, but I didn't believe I deserved it. Yet, even in my darkest moments, God was there, patiently waiting for me to see that He had been fighting for me all along. This book is my journey—through pain, through doubt, through the lies of fear—and into the truth of God's love and power. It's not just a recounting of events; it's a testimony of transformation. It's about how I found hope in the midst of hopelessness, and how I discovered that the chains that bound me were never unbreakable—they were illusions that dissolved the moment I fully trusted God to take the wheel.

I write this not to dwell on the pain but to shine a light on the path to freedom. If you've ever felt trapped, hopeless, or powerless, I hope my story reminds you that freedom is possible. That God is bigger than fear. And that your story isn't over—because with Him, it's never too late to begin again. This is my journey, but it's also an invitation for you to start yours. Let's walk this path together, leaving fear behind and stepping into the fullness of what God has for us.

ACKNOWLEDGMENTS

First and foremost, I give all thanks and glory to my Heavenly Father. Lord, my gratitude for You cannot be captured in words—there simply aren't enough words to express the depth of my love for You. Your unfailing love, mercy, and grace have transformed me and made me who I am today. This book is a testament to Your power, Your presence, and the miracles You have worked in my life. Thank You for loving me, even when I didn't know how to love myself, and for never letting go of me, even when I tried to run away.

I want to thank my sons, who have always been my biggest cheerleaders and my unwavering source of strength. Your belief in me has carried me through every achievement and reminded me of why I continue to push forward. You are my greatest blessings, and I am forever grateful for the love and pride you show me every day.

To my spiritual mother, thank you for introducing me to my Lord and Savior and for being a living example of what it means to be a strong prayer warrior. Your faith, wisdom, and unshakable trust in God have inspired me to stand firm in every storm. You have been a guiding light, and I am eternally grateful for your presence in my life.

To my husband, thank you for your steadfast support and love as I poured my heart into writing this book. You have shown me what it truly means to be loved, respected, and supported unconditionally. Your encouragement has been a pillar of strength for me, and I am so blessed to walk this journey with you by my side.

I want to take a moment to express my deepest gratitude to my spiritual leader, Apostle Bryan Andrew Wilson. Thank you for your guidance, your love, and your PUSH! Your leadership and unwavering faith have been a source of inspiration, strength, and transformation in my life.

Thank you for allowing God to show you ME! For seeing beyond the surface, for speaking life into my purpose, and for leading with wisdom, compassion, and power. From the very moment I stepped into Freedom of Atlanta, I knew I had found HOME!

I appreciate your covering, your prayers, and your commitment to God's calling. May the Lord continue to bless, strengthen, and elevate you, expanding your territory and bringing forth every vision He has placed in your heart.

To every woman who has endured abuse, this book is for you, too. Society may call us survivors when we break free, but the Word of God declares that you are so much more—you are more than a conqueror. You can overcome, you can conquer, and you can step into the fullness of the life God has for you. It's okay to love again, to trust again, and to hope again. Hold firm to the words: "Fear not, for I am with you" (Isaiah 41:10), and know that He is God. May you find strength, peace, and the courage to walk boldly into your future, knowing that you are not just surviving—you are thriving.

CONTENTS

Introduction 13

Chapter 1
Stepping Into the Truth 15

Chapter 2
Behind Closed Doors 21

Chapter 3
The Lie of Fear 54

Chapter4
The Power of Unwavering Faith 121

Chapter 5
Fear.. 127

Chapter 6
Fitted Feet 142

Chapter 7
Prayer 149

About the Author 175

INTRODUCTION

Have you ever felt trapped by fear, weighed down by heartbreak, or convinced that you had to face life's battles alone? If so, this book is for you. Within these pages, you will find the raw, transparent testimony of someone who has walked through abuse, loss, and despair—only to discover that God was there all along, ready and willing to deliver. You will read about the journey from bondage to boldness, from depression to determination, and from doubt to an unshakeable faith. You will witness how God's Word, prayer, and a genuine surrender led to a life transformed—one marked by love, grace, peace, and courage.

Throughout this book, I share personal experiences of suffering, spiritual warfare, and the relentless whispers of fear that once kept me bound. More importantly, you'll see how God brought me out, step by step, and equipped me with the armor to silence the enemy's lies. It wasn't an overnight miracle but a powerful process—one that shaped me into a prayer warrior, a bolder believer, and a testimony of God's faithfulness. My hope is that by reading this story, you'll be inspired to shut down fear in your own life and step confidently into the promises God has for you. If God can do it for me—trust me—He can (and will) do it for you. Come along, dive in, and discover how to exchange fear for faith, bondage for freedom, and heartbreak for hope. Your story isn't over; this is only the beginning.

CHAPTER 1

STEPPING INTO THE TRUTH

WHO GOD SAYS WE ARE

When I first considered writing a book, my initial thought was simple: I would share the story of my life and how God saved me from countless tragedies. I imagined laying out the details, chapter by chapter, and letting readers see His hand in my journey. But as the years went by, each time I sat down to write, I would start and then stop. Something always held me back. Looking back now, I think I always knew deep down that I wasn't truly ready to tell my story—not because I lacked experiences to share, but because I felt my story needed to be more than just a recounting of events. It needed to serve a greater purpose, to speak to something deeper than what happened in my life. It needed to resonate with others, to inspire, and to reflect the lessons God has woven into my journey.

Until I could write with that clarity and intention, I knew the time wasn't right. I mean, sure, I could tell you that I am a survivor of rape, of molestation, of years of physical and psychological abuse—but honestly, many women can tell you the same thing. So, really, what is the purpose? What is my purpose, and more importantly, what is God's purpose in all of it? It's not enough for me to simply recount the pain I've endured or the battles I've fought. My story has to be about more than survival—it has to be about redemption, healing, and the ways God can transform even the deepest wounds into something meaningful. I've come to realize that the real power in my story lies in the "why" and the "how": Why did God carry me through it all? And how can my journey become a source of hope for someone else? God doesn't waste pain, and He doesn't allow us to walk through the fire without a reason. Maybe His purpose is to remind others that no matter how broken they feel, there is a path to healing and restoration. Maybe my purpose is to be a living testament to His grace, His love, and His ability to bring life out of death. Whatever the answer, I know it's about more than just me—it's about letting God's light shine through the darkest parts of my story. One thing I am sure of is that I want to share with you how fear kept me more bound than any abuse I ever suffered.

Fear is a lie—a deceptive, consuming lie that whispers you'll never be free, never be whole, never be enough. I want to talk to you about the Lie of Fear. I used to think of fear as something powerful, something that had control over me. But as I've grown and healed, I've come to realize that fear has no real power unless you give it permission. It's like a shadow—daunting only when you let it loom over you. Fear fed on my pain, on my silence, and on the belief that I wasn't strong enough to face it. But the truth is, fear is powerless against faith. It's powerless against truth. And once I started to confront fear for what it was—a lie designed to keep me from stepping into my purpose—I began to see the freedom on the other side. My hope is to share with you how I broke free from the chains of fear, and how you can, too. Because once you stop feeding fear, it starves. Once you shine a light on it, it shrinks. And once you trust God to replace fear with courage, you begin to see the life you were created to live. So, this story isn't just about survival—it's about victory over the lies that try to keep us bound. It's about stepping into the truth of who God says we are: not victims, not captives, but conquerors.

Throughout my journey, I have wrestled with countless questions. I questioned my purpose. I questioned the reasons behind the trauma I endured. What could possibly be the purpose of experiencing so much pain, especially as a child? Why would God allow such things to happen to me? I questioned whether I had somehow brought these assaults upon myself. Was there something about me that provoked such terrible behavior in others? As a child, how could I have possibly done anything to invite such acts? Was it the way I dressed, the things I said, or the way I carried myself? I wondered if my smile or my outspoken, sassy attitude had somehow made me a target.

Growing up, I spent more time around adults than children. Maybe I came across as too mature for my age, too bold, too confident, and that somehow invited these horrible actions from the perpetrators in my life. The weight of these questions stayed with me for years. I tried to make sense of what seemed senseless, searching for a reason that might help me understand why these events had marked my life so deeply. My very first encounter with Fear happened at a very young age. I was five, maybe six. My mom was a single parent, doing her best to provide for us, working wherever she could. Her jobs often stretched past the hours when school let out, so I was left to my own devices for a few hours each day. I was that kid—the one who hung out on the block, known by everyone.

There was the neighbor up the street who kept pet tarantulas in glass tanks, a fascination that sent shivers down my spine. Then there was the taxi cab driver across the street, always with a smile and a wave. The taxi cab stand was my regular hangout as Rosey, the dispatcher, would sit me on her lap and let me speak to the taxi drivers over the radio. Next door to us, there was the family-owned real estate office: husband, wife, and their two adult children. Everyone on the block seemed to know me, and I felt safe in the familiarity of it all. To a child, the world feels smaller, more manageable, when you're surrounded by faces you recognize. I didn't know then how quickly that sense of safety could be shattered, how innocence could be stripped away in a single moment. The realtor's office was one of my favorite places to visit. The wife was kind and had a way of making me feel important. She'd let me sit at the big desk, tapping away on an old black typewriter, pretending I was her secretary. I loved those moments, playing dress-up in a world of grown-ups, feeling like I belonged. But one day, everything changed.

One day, it wasn't the wife or the cheerful chatter of the office that greeted me. It was the husband. He was there alone. That day, Fear introduced itself to me for the first time. My memory of that day is fragmented, like a broken mirror reflecting pieces of something too painful to hold all at once. But some parts are so very clear. I remember the big brown leather couch, its texture and smell etched into my mind. I remember being alone with him, and I remember seeing and feeling a part of this man's physical anatomy that no child should ever have to encounter as he lay over my small body and violated my innocence. What happened afterward? I couldn't tell you. That part is a haze.

The actual details of the act are blurred, shrouded in a fog that my mind refuses to lift. But I can tell you with certainty that he took a part of me not only physically but mentally that scarred me and opened up the door to a world of fear that I would reside in for many years to come. When the memories of that day first started surfacing, they came with an overwhelming wave of disgust and dread. It was as though the violation lived in the pit of my stomach, manifesting as an unbearable weight that I could feel even without a clear recollection of the specifics. What I do know is what didn't happen—I wasn't rescued by anyone. There was no call to the police. There was no one to stop this assault. I could take the blame and say that nothing happened to save me or bring forth justice simply because I didn't say a word. How could I? How does a six-year-old even begin to articulate something so incomprehensible? How do you find the words to explain something you can barely process yourself?

At that age, the weight of confusion and fear silences you, locking away the truth in a vault you don't yet have the tools to open. That day remained seared into my mental photo album—a haunting image I could not erase. It was the day I met the Lie of Fear. Fear whispered to me, convincing me to stay silent, to lock away the truth deep inside. It told me that opening my mouth to speak would bring nothing but confusion and disbelief. "No one will understand," it said. "You don't even understand it yourself."

And Fear was right about one thing—I didn't fully grasp what had happened to me. I only knew it was wrong, that it felt dark and heavy, that it was something too terrible to put into words. Fear wrapped its chains around my voice, silencing me before I ever had the chance to cry out. Looking back, I realize how deeply that lie burrowed into my soul, wrapping itself around me like chains. Fear didn't just silence me in that moment—it planted seeds that would grow into years of self-doubt, shame, and mistrust. That day wasn't just the day I was violated; it was the day I learned how fear can hold you captive, even long after the moment has passed.

CHAPTER 2

BEHIND CLOSED DOORS

A FALSE SENSE OF FAMILY

My mom was a single parent until I was about eight years old. She was also a recovering alcoholic, and I spent countless hours sitting with her in AA meetings. To this day, I could tell you exactly where those meetings were held and when they took place. Those people became like a second family to me. I remember many nights falling asleep on someone's lap while the room buzzed with voices sharing their stories of struggle and hope. And yes, I was a bit spoiled. There was always someone who made sure I had a cold glass of milk and a slice of crumb cake at every meeting.

My mother's sponsor, Anee, and her husband, Don, always came bearing gifts. It became a ritual, something I looked forward to while my mom focused on her recovery. It was at one of those meetings—a Wednesday night gathering—that my mom met my stepfather. At first, he seemed like a genuinely nice man. Polite, funny, and attentive, he carried himself in a way that made it easy to trust him. My mom, who had spent so much time focusing on herself and her sobriety, began to spend more and more time with him and less and less time in those meetings.

For her, he must have seemed like a fresh start, a chance at companionship and stability. For me, it was the beginning of a chapter I could never have imagined, one that would take us down a path far from the hope and peace she had been working so hard to achieve. It all happened so fast. Before I could even process what was going on, she sat me down and told me we were moving in with him. And not long after that, she mentioned they'd be getting married. I was eight years old at the time. This was the first time my spidey sense—that gut feeling we all have—screamed at me. He seemed nice enough, and he even did those "dad things" that should've made me feel secure. But the moment she said we'd be living with him, I felt something deep inside me tighten.

A sense of unease washed over me, though I couldn't put words to it then. I wanted to trust my mom's judgment. I wanted to believe that everything would be okay, that this man would be the father figure I didn't have. But my instincts wouldn't let me fully accept it. Something felt off, and even as a child, I knew better than to ignore that feeling. Well, Spidey was on point. Not long after we moved in, my mom stopped going to AA meetings. Those rooms filled with support and hope were replaced by bottles and chaos. Both of them began drinking heavily, and the man who once seemed like the dad I never had quickly transformed into a nightmare—one that lasted for seven long years.

At first, my stepdad seemed like a dream come true. He taught me how to ride my first bike, brought home a puppy just for me, and always had me by his side as he worked on cars, patiently showing me the basics of tools and car parts. For a moment, it felt like I had the kind of father figure every child dreams of—a protector, a teacher, someone who cared about me. But what seemed wonderful at first always found its way back to punishment. When the puppy became too much for me to manage at just eight years old, my stepdad put it in the car, drove out of the neighborhood, and left it on the street. I never saw it again. Then, he brought home a poodle, but when that dog didn't take well to my attempts at handling it—snipping and snapping at me—it too disappeared, never to return. There was no understanding of my age and my inability to train this dog. There was only punishment for failing to do so.

The same pattern followed with my bike. It was taken away the moment I did something that upset him. Even the friends next door, the one bright spot of connection in my life, were stripped away. He didn't approve of the color of their skin, and just like that, I was forbidden from playing with them. What started as gestures of kindness and care were always twisted into tools of control, teaching me that anything good could be snatched away at a moment's notice. At just eight years old, I began wetting the bed.

The first time my stepfather discovered it, his reaction was not one of comfort or understanding but of anger. I was beaten with a wooden paddle, a belt, or stick and punished for the rest of the day. The fear that night instilled in me never left. From then on, every time I woke up to a damp bed, panic consumed me. I was terrified of what would happen if I was caught again. I was just a small child, yet I found myself struggling to lift my mattress—desperately flipping it over to hide the evidence, hoping that he would not discover what I had done. It became a secret battle, one that I faced alone in the dark, driven by fear rather than the reassurance and care that every child deserves. There isn't a single memory that has faded. I remember the first inappropriate touch—his hands crossing boundaries no child should ever endure.

The first time this happened, my mother had an argument with him. She stormed out of the house, leaving me behind. I remember as he sat at the window with me standing beside him, how she came into the yard looking for me as if she knew herself that leaving me with him was a bad decision. She didn't come back to get me, and at that moment, he decided it was time to start touching parts of me that no father should even consider. I remember that feeling of fear because I had encountered it before. While still being very young, I couldn't comprehend fully what and why this was happening, but I knew it was dark, it was bad, and it was not a form of love but of harm. I remember the first beating with wooden sticks, the sting and bruises lasting far longer than the physical pain. I remember the humiliation when he cut off all my hair because I couldn't keep it from tangling, as though my struggles as a child were something I should be punished for. And then there was the first time I saw him hit my mother—a moment that shattered what little sense of safety I clung to. That day is seared into my mind.

My mom was pregnant with my sister, probably around eight months along. They were arguing—loud and angry—

but that wasn't unusual. What came next was. From my bedroom, I heard her screams. Terrified, I ran to see what was happening. When I reached the room, I froze. He was sitting on her swollen belly, strangling her with both hands. Her face was red and panicked, her breath coming in shallow gasps. I didn't know what to do. Fear gripped me, but I couldn't stand there and do nothing. So, I ran. I ran out the door, all the way to the corner bar where the regulars knew my stepfather's name. I begged them to save her, the words tumbling out through sobs. I hid under the bar, shaking with fear that he'd come after me for telling, for trying to stop him. The police came, but it didn't matter. My mom denied everything, and nothing changed. When we got back home, I was punished—not him. I was beaten and then locked in my room, left to sit with my fear, my guilt for telling anyone, and my helplessness.

That night, I learned that fear isn't just about being hurt. It's about the silence it forces on you, the way it tells you that no one will believe you, that no one will protect you, that you are utterly and completely alone. The abuse didn't stop there. Much of the physical abuse fell squarely on me. But it wasn't the bruises or the beatings that scarred me the most—it was the sexual abuse. In my mind, that was the ultimate violation, the worst thing a person could endure. I dreaded every moment my mother left me alone with him. During those times, I was subjected to sexual actions that violated my personal boundaries and well-being. If I resisted, he would retaliate with punishments, taking away things I valued deeply—my toys, access to television, and what little interaction I had with other children and even my own siblings and mother. He used these as tools of control, granting them only when I complied with his expectations.

My most precious possession—the one thing I longed for most—was my mother. Yet, he controlled our access to each other and kept me from her, not by physical chains but through manipulation and restriction. Though we lived under the same roof, he ensured that my time was either spent with him or in solitude. There were no mother-daughter outings, no shared moments of closeness, not even casual time together within the home. He made sure of that. I no longer had the mother who read bedtime stories to me or pretended to be my favorite TV characters as she changed her voice to sound like them at the dinner table as a form of play with me. I no longer had the mother who took me to the park or made my Halloween costumes by hand so I could take part in the festivities at school or go trick-or-treating with her. He stripped this away. His jealousy was suffocating, but perhaps, even more than that, he was afraid. Afraid that if I had too much time with her, I might whisper the truth—the horrors that took place in the middle of the night, the early mornings, and the moments when she was away at work or simply running an errand. And so, she was made off-limits to me.

The one person who should have been my safe place was kept just out of reach, not by her own doing but by his calculated control. Well, yes, by her own doing as well because she submitted to him even when it meant hurting me. I say this because there was a night that he woke me up out of my sleep with his hands pulling down my panties. I wanted him to stop, leave me alone, so I found a moment of courage to run to my mother's bed to try to tell her I was being violated. Now, my mother was hard of hearing and wore a hearing aid. She would take this off at night, and so hearing anything was pretty limited, BUT she could see. I stood before her with my panties still around my ankles, crying and trying to put together the right words to tell her what he was doing. I remember her looking at me with wide eyes, but instead of jumping up in outrage of what I was showing her, she yelled at me, got up, and yelled at him to leave me alone and let me go to bed because I had school in the morning. That was it!! There nothing more! And the nothing more spoke loudly to me. She wasn't going to save me!

So, even though I continued to express an intention to disclose his behavior, he escalated his threats and warned me of severe consequences, including taking my mother's life. He claimed that speaking out would result in harm to my family and the separation of my siblings into foster care. I knew then that my cry for help was falling on deaf ears. As a child, these threats created a deep sense of fear and helplessness, leaving me feeling trapped and uncertain about how to protect myself or seek help. This experience left an indelible mark on me, shaping my understanding of fear, manipulation, and the impact of unchecked authority. He didn't stay within the bounds of inappropriate touching for long. He escalated, taking my innocence and replacing it with shame, confusion, and fear.

The man who was supposed to be my protector—my father

figure—became my violator. He became all the things that kill, steal, and destroy, wrapped up in one person. As if that weren't bad enough, the physical punishments came just as easily. Beatings for peeing the bed. Beatings for not washing the dishes to his standards. Beatings for wanting to play with friends who weren't white. It seemed like everything I did was wrong, like my very existence was a constant offense. I learned quickly that my survival depended on pleasing him in every way. If I didn't, the consequences were swift and brutal. And so, I lived in a constant state of walking on eggshells, trying to predict what would set him off next, trying to find some way to avoid the pain. But the truth is, there was no pleasing him. There was no escape. No matter how hard I tried, I was always at his mercy, and mercy was something he never seemed to have. And as if everything I endured at home wasn't bad enough, the horrors didn't stop there. I met this sin—this act of disgust—not just from my stepdad but from others as well.

My stepdad was a machinist by trade, and he had a fully equipped workshop set up in the back of the house. He spent hours making tools and selling them to workers at the egg factory down the road. And guess who he used as his delivery person? Me. I still remember José, one of the mechanics at the factory who worked alongside his son. The very first time I delivered a tool to him, instead of gratitude, he delivered groping and grabbing as his twisted version of a thank-you. I was only 10 or 11 years old. The shame and confusion hit me like a wave I didn't know how to swim against. I didn't know how to say no. I didn't even know if I could say no. Then there were the Sunday mornings.

Every week, I was sent to the store to buy the newspaper and some hard rolls for breakfast. My stepdad gave me a strict time to return home, and if I was even a minute late, I knew there would be hell to pay. On my way to the store, I would pass the laundromat that sat between the old Food Town and the bakery. Every Sunday, I would see the old man who worked there. He seemed kind, innocent even. To my young, naive mind, he felt safe. Talking to him became a tiny window into normalcy, a rare chance to socialize, however brief. This meant the world to me because at home, I had no one. My stepdad didn't allow friends to visit, I wasn't permitted to talk on the phone, and the doors were locked with so many deadbolts that the house felt like a prison. Even my bedroom window was nailed shut, leaving just an inch or two for air to seep in.

On those sweltering summer nights, my room became a furnace. I can still feel the sticky, sweat-soaked linen clinging to my skin, the air heavy and stale as the box fan hummed uselessly in the corner. It was unbearable, isolating, suffocating. So, when the old man at the laundromat smiled at me and struck up a conversation, it felt like a gift. But I was wrong. What began as innocent chatter quickly turned into something sinister. His kind demeanor masked an insidious intent. His words became inappropriate, his actions invasive. It felt like I was surrounded by predators, trapped in a world where my safety and innocence didn't matter. Every interaction became a question of survival. How could I stay invisible enough to escape harm, yet present enough to not make things worse?

It was a tightrope walk I didn't sign up for, and the cost of falling off was everything. By the age of 13, I found the strength to say no. No to his inappropriate demands. No to the violation of my body. No to the sickening control he had over my life. But that act of defiance, of reclaiming a small piece of my dignity, came at a price—a price I was willing to pay as long as it meant he wouldn't touch me, wouldn't take from me, wouldn't force himself on me anymore. What followed wasn't freedom; it was a new kind of torment. He traded one form of abuse for another. The beatings came swiftly and for the most absurd reasons. If the school bus was late, I was punished. If a dish wasn't spotless, I was beaten. Every minor infraction became an excuse to unleash his rage. And then there were the nights. Many nights, he would sit drunk at the kitchen table, a shadow of the man he pretended to be to the outside world. I'd be startled awake by the shock of ice-cold water thrown in my face. "Get up," he'd slur, ordering me to sit with him until the morning light, forcing me to endure his drunken ramblings while exhaustion clawed at me. I would then drag myself to school, sleep-deprived and broken. Even the most basic necessities became tools of his cruelty.

Bathing was rationed, restricted to once a week, as though cleanliness was a privilege I didn't deserve. Clean clothes were sparse, distributed on a schedule he controlled with no regard for my needs. And when he decided I "smelled like an animal," he would send me to the woods with nothing but a roll of toilet paper to relieve myself. This memory has left a permanent imprint on my mind. I remember walking across the road toward the woods, my head heavy with shame and my heart pounding with fear. What awaited me in those woods? As a child, I often wondered about the people I had seen entering and exiting the woods. Who were they? Would they harm me if I encountered them? The unknown terrified me, but so did the humiliation of facing his taunts if I tried to use the bathroom at home.

Many times, I tried to endure the stomach pains, ignoring my body's needs just to avoid the woods and his relentless insults. Sadly enough, I wasn't always successful and would find myself in the bathroom at school, trying to bathe myself and scrub my panties clean to avoid smelling and being teased by my classmates. Here's the cruel irony—though I feared the woods and the unknown dangers that might lurk within them, I also found solace in their isolation. For a fleeting moment, they provided an escape from home, a place where I could breathe, even if only briefly. But somehow, as if he sensed this, he found a way to taint that, too. He began taking me on so-called "trips" into the woods—under the guise of spending time with me. But I knew the truth. There was nothing innocent about his intentions.

There, surrounded by nothing but trees and silence, he would attempt to touch me, and I would resist. And, of course, my refusal always came with consequences—I knew that all too well. One morning, his need for control intertwined with his addiction. At 6 a.m., he forced me to walk nearly two miles with him to a corner bar, a place where he could drown himself in alcohol without shame. Just across from that bar was a park. And in his twisted mind, he convinced himself that this was a father-daughter outing—quality time, as if his presence in that park somehow erased the horror of his actions. I remember him sitting there, looking me in the eye and confessing that what he had done to me was wrong. But then, in the same breath, he justified it. "It's different," he said, "because you're not my biological child." *What?! Dude—I am a child! What part of that is missing in your head?*

How could he twist reality so deeply that he thought this was something that could be explained away? As if biology had anything to do with the violation of innocence. As if his admission, drenched in excuses, could somehow make it right. It was in that moment, sitting in that park, that I realized just how truly broken his mind was. And yet, somehow, I was the one left carrying the weight of his sins. As I reflect on my childhood, the beatings, isolation, and sexual assaults stand out as undeniably traumatic. However, for many who have endured similar experiences, it's often the "other things"—the small, daily humiliations—that leave lasting scars. For me, these memories are just as vivid, and they shaped much of how I saw myself and the world. We were a poor family. My stepfather rarely worked, and when he did, it was never for long.

My mother worked part-time, but her earnings barely scratched the surface of what we needed. Food often came from pantries and churches, and I vividly remember the government-issued cheese that was a staple in our home. While food was sparse, clothing was an entirely different struggle. My mother would take me to charities for hand-me-downs, but the clothes she brought home were rarely age-appropriate. Often, they were garments better suited for much older women. Shoes were either too small, too worn, or entirely impractical for a child my age. One memory that has lingered was the humiliation of going to school wearing a torn pair of baseball cleats, patched together by my stepfather with electrical tape. Fear gripped me on my way to school that day, and by the time I reached gym class, the inevitable ridicule from classmates reduced me to tears. The laughter echoed as I ran out of the gym, retreating to the bathroom, overwhelmed by shame and embarrassment. It wasn't just the poverty; it was the deliberate disregard for my needs that cemented my understanding that, to my stepfather, I had no value. I became desperate to fit in, to avoid the cruelty of my peers.

Late at night, I would sit in my room with a needle and thread, painstakingly altering the bell-bottom pants I was forced to wear, trying to make them look more like the clothes other kids wore. It was a small rebellion, a grasp for normalcy in a life that felt anything but. One evening, as I sat by my bedroom window, I saw my neighbor throwing away a pair of burgundy leather ankle boots. To me, it was as though I had struck gold. I waited until she went back inside and then raced to retrieve them from the trash. They were slightly too big and a bit worn, but I didn't care. To me, they were the most beautiful shoes I had ever owned. I wore them proudly, even as the soles began to wear thin, because for the first time in a long while, I felt a sense of pride and belonging, however fleeting it may have been. These moments, as painful and humiliating as they were, taught me resilience. They showed me how to find joy in small victories, even in the face of hardship. But they also serve as a reminder of how deeply neglect and disregard can wound a child's spirit. The first time I made my own money, I was just 11 years old. My stepfather, surprisingly, allowed it, which was unusual given his typical control over every aspect of my life. The opportunity came from the elderly widow across the street, whose husband had recently passed away. That winter, after the first big snowfall, she asked if I could shovel her driveway and offered to pay me $20.

Back in the '80s, $20 was a lot of money for a child. I was astonished when my stepfather agreed, but I didn't question it—I grabbed the shovel and got to work. That $20 felt like a fortune to me, and for the first time, I experienced a taste of independence. With my earnings, I went straight to the clearance rack at Bradlees and bought my very first pair of designer jeans. I couldn't believe it—I had something new, something of quality, and most importantly, something I had earned myself. I cherished those jeans, wearing them at every chance I got. When the thighs eventually wore out, I refused to give them up. I carefully sewed the holes and kept wearing them, proud of my first purchase and what it represented. It wasn't just about the jeans—it was about what they symbolized: my ability to create something better for myself, even in small ways. That moment planted a seed in me, a desire for independence and self-sufficiency, and it was a feeling I held on to tightly.

My very first job was at Caldor when I was just 14 years old. My mother had managed to convince my stepfather to allow me to work there, largely because she also worked at the store. It felt like a small victory. I made $65 a week—a modest amount, but to me, it was a lifeline to independence. Of course, my stepfather made sure to take a large portion of my earnings, arguing that I needed to contribute to the household. Despite this, I cherished what little was left. It gave me the ability to treat myself, even if it was just something off the clearance rack once or twice a month. Those small purchases were more than just material items—they were symbols of freedom, however fleeting. But, as always, he found ways to make my life difficult.

Despite my mother also working at Caldor, she never offered to drive me home, nor did he allow it. Instead, I was forced to walk home alone late at night, a journey that stretched at least three miles. If I wasn't home on time, the doors were locked. That's just how it was. I spent many nights outside, wandering the streets until sunrise. I'd curl up on park benches or huddle in the back doorway of my family's home, hoping someone would let me in. Strangely, one of the places I found myself seeking refuge was the graveyard. I know what you're thinking—*What kind of person chooses to sleep in a graveyard?* But there was an odd peace about it. In my young mind, it made sense. Who would bother me there? It felt safer than the streets. So, I'd sit quietly among the headstones, waiting for the first rays of morning light.

Looking back, I can't help but laugh a little at my younger self—finding solace in such an unconventional place. But the truth is, those moments taught me resilience. They showed me that even in the most unusual circumstances, I could find a way to endure. So, don't judge me too harshly—chalk it up to youthful survival instincts and maybe just a dash of teenage ingenuity! Winter nights were always the hardest. Snow blanketed the ground, and the temperatures often plunged into the negatives. Those nights outside, with nothing but my own breath to keep me company, were brutal. All because a school bus ran late, or I took a few extra minutes walking home in the rain or snow after work, or I spent too long at the checkout counter running errands for him. His punishments never seemed to fit the "crimes," and they always ended with me locked out in the cold.

One particular morning stands out in my memory—a turning point, really. It was 6 a.m., and I had been outside all night, shivering as the icy wind pierced through my thin coat. I just wanted to go to school. I needed my clothing, my books, and, frankly, just a bit of warmth. So, I banged on the door, desperate for a chance to get inside. When he opened the door, his face was twisted with anger. He cursed at me and told me to get lost. But that day, something inside me snapped. I had endured enough. I called the police. When they arrived, I explained everything—my age, his unreasonable punishments, and why I was being left out in the freezing cold. My stepfather, confident that the police would side with him, told his version of the story with the same arrogance he used to enforce his punishments. But his confidence was misplaced.

The officers listened, and after delivering a very stern warning to him, they ensured I would not spend another night outside—not until the day I finally left that house for good. That moment didn't just bring warmth to my frozen fingers; it brought a flicker of hope. It was the first time someone had intervened, the first time I felt that maybe, just maybe, I didn't have to endure it all alone. It was a small victory, but one that gave me strength to keep pushing forward, even on the coldest of nights. This wasn't just physical abuse—it was psychological warfare, calculated to humiliate, degrade, and dehumanize me at every turn. It stripped away my dignity and replaced it with a constant state of fear and shame, leaving scars far deeper than the physical ones. School should have been a safe haven, but it was anything but that. Kids didn't understand what I was enduring.

All they saw was a disheveled, unkempt girl who smelled bad and didn't fit in. The bullies thrived off of my appearance and turned me into their favorite target. Their laughter and cruel words were like daggers, cutting into what little self-worth I had left. At that point, I wasn't sure what I feared more: going to school or staying at home. Both felt like prisons, each with its own kind of torment. But strangely, school became a refuge of sorts. As harsh as it was, it was still a place where he wasn't. It wasn't freedom, but it was the closest thing to it I had. And in those moments away from his grasp, I clung to the faint hope that one day, I'd find a way out of this nightmare. One day, I'd be free. Now, here's the crazy thing: Through all of this pain, chaos, and heartbreak, I knew God existed. I believed in Jesus Christ. I believed, or at least hoped, that one day, He would save me.

That one day, He would reach down into the mess of my

life and pull me out. We weren't a church-going family, not by any stretch, but before my mom married the man who became my nightmare, she taught me about Jesus. She told me He loved me. She told me He died for me. Those were powerful words for a child to hear, even though I didn't fully understand them at the time. I clung to them like a lifeline, a fragile thread of hope that somehow kept me tethered to the idea that there was something greater than the brokenness I lived in. I can still remember some of the stories my mom told me when I was little. We'd be walking home, and if the sun's rays pierced through the clouds just right, she'd smile and say, "That's God's eyes shining down on you." Those moments were fleeting but powerful. They planted seeds of hope in me—hope in a Father I didn't yet know but longed to believe in. Those stories, those glimpses of light, built in me a love and a longing for a God who seemed so far away. In the midst of everything I endured, it was that hope, that faint belief in His existence, that gave me the strength to hold on when all I wanted to do was let go. I didn't know Him personally then, but I trusted that somehow, someday, I would. And that hope was enough to keep me going. For most of my childhood, I endured abuse from a man who wore the label of "father."

I often escaped into fantasies about my biological father coming back to rescue me from this nightmare. I imagined him swooping in, shielding me from harm, and finally being the protector I so desperately needed. But those fantasies always ended with a deep anger. My father had been absent since I was a baby, making no effort to be the man I thought he should be—a protector, a provider, a model of what a good man looks like. Little did I know that I already had exactly what I longed for in my Heavenly Father. I wouldn't realize this truth until many years later. But at the time, I felt alone, unprotected, and completely drained of hope. By the time I was 15, something in me had reached its breaking point.

On this particular day, I had heard my last insult. I had endured my last beating, my last punishment, and my last moment of being told I was worthless, would always be nothing, and deserved even less. I remember the moment vividly. As he spewed his venomous words at me, degrading me, something inside me snapped. I couldn't take another second of it. Without thinking, I walked into his bedroom, pulled open the bottom drawer of his dresser, and grabbed that shiny piece of metal I knew held bullets. My mind wasn't clear; it was filled with anger, pain, and a desperation I'd never felt before. I walked out of the room, the weight of the object in my hand feeling like the only power I had left, heading straight for him. And then my mother stepped into the hallway. She stopped me. She didn't say a word, but she knew. She could see it in my face, and I could see in hers that she understood exactly what I was about to do. In that moment, something shifted. I realized that if I didn't leave, if I stayed in that house, I might not survive. I didn't know where I would go or what I would do, but I knew I had to go. I am sure many reading would have the thought of, *Why did your mother not protect you?*

Well, while I cannot excuse her for not protecting me from harm, I can tell you that God has shown me her own bondage and how that bondage kept her from standing up against the abuse I endured. My mother, up until the age of 14, was drugged, raped, and exploited through child pornagraphy by her own father. This left her bound in fear, lack of self-worth, and drowning in addiction and codependency. Does this excuse her? No! Does it explain to me that she was in her own darkness and needed saving? Yes! I wish I could tell you that the moment I walked out of my stepfather's house, I never returned. But that wouldn't be true. Life after leaving wasn't a straight road to freedom or safety. I stayed with friends when I could, often slept outside, and many nights, I didn't sleep at all. Eventually, out of sheer desperation, I ended up renting a room in the basement of my stepfather's house—a decision born not of choice but necessity. That basement wasn't just a room; it was a dwelling for rats, roaches, and a sewage system that backed up every time it rained. It wasn't shelter; it was survival. As disgusting as it sounds, that grimy basement taught me something profound—it humbled me. It was in that dark, damp, infested space that I first felt the tiniest inkling of independence, of being on my own, a fragile sense of something that was my own.

It wasn't much, but it was mine. But don't misunderstand; my stepfather didn't relinquish control just because I lived below ground. He found new ways to remind me of his power. If he suspected I had a visitor, he would padlock the front door, effectively trapping me. He cut the wires to the phone I paid for, ensuring I couldn't communicate with the outside world. His insults and venomous words didn't stop, either—he screamed them down the basement stairs as if his voice could reach even the lowest depths of my soul. And yet, in the midst of all of this, there was a flicker of hope. For a brief moment, I felt free—not entirely, but enough. Enough to know I was no longer completely in his grasp. Enough to know that I was starting to take small steps toward something better, even if I didn't yet know what that "better" was. We often ask God the hard questions, especially when it comes to the suffering of children. How could a loving God allow such pain—whether through abuse, sickness, or circumstances that seem far from just? Where is the justice for them? Why aren't they healed, or, better yet, spared from suffering altogether? These are not easy questions to grapple with.

In my search for answers, I recently met with my Apostle, hoping to find clarity, wisdom, and perhaps a way to bring you a word that might make sense of it all. He shared examples of David, Joseph, and even Jesus with me; he provided me with understanding of how they, too, suffered as young men. I held on tightly to the story of Jesus and how even as a newborn infant, the sin of man planned for suffering and death. Joseph was hated by his own siblings and sold into slavery. David also endured many hardships and dangers as a young boy. But let's go back to Jesus. What on earth did he do to cause the king to want him dead? Nothing at all. It was the king's sinful nature that saw Jesus as a threat to his own selfish desires. When thinking about this, Jesus endured a suffering and a death that cannot truly be described in words FOR ME!!! I also thought, God could have stopped all of it, but there was a greater purpose to come from Jesus's pain.

As I said earlier, God doesn't waste your pain. Here is what I've come to understand: Not everything is meant for our comprehension. Some truths lie beyond the scope of human understanding. And as hard as it may be to hear, we must also acknowledge a fundamental truth—humanity, not God, birthed sin. God created a beginning for us that was free from pain, free from suffering. He gave us a perfect garden, a perfect relationship with Him, and the freedom to choose. It is in that freedom that sin entered the world—not by God's doing, but by human choice. Now, let me be clear: God did not create the perversion I endured as a child. God did not compel my abusers to choose the paths they did. Those were their choices, born from a world marred by sin, not by God's hand. But what I'm about to share might seem outrageous at first—it's something I've come to realize about my own life.

Looking back, not just on my childhood but on every part of my journey, I can say this with conviction: What I endured made me who I am. Don't misunderstand me—this isn't to say that what happened was right or just. It wasn't. But I've come to see how the trials I faced, the pain I endured, shaped me into a person who can now speak to you from a place of understanding, empathy, and strength. God didn't create the suffering, but He has used it to mold me, to refine me, to give me a testimony that can inspire hope in others. Through my struggles, I've learned to lean on God, to trust Him even when the "why" remains unanswered. And while I may never fully understand why some suffer as they do, I know this: God's love, grace, and power are bigger than any pain. He promises to walk with us through the darkest valleys, to turn what was meant for evil into something good, and to give us strength when we feel we have none. So, while the suffering of children—and anyone, for that matter—may never fully make sense to us, we can rest in the truth that God is not the author of their pain. He is the healer, the redeemer, and the one who can bring beauty from the ashes.

The stories of Joseph, David, and Jesus each tell a profound journey of suffering, hardship, and eventual triumph, demonstrating God's sovereignty over human circumstances and His ultimate plans for redemption. Joseph's journey is one of betrayal, loss, and injustice. He was sold by his brothers and wrongfully imprisoned, and yet, he rose to a place of prominence in Egypt, where he was able to save many lives, including those of his family. The outcome of Joseph's journey wasn't just about personal success but about fulfilling God's greater purpose. Despite the deep pain he endured, he ultimately declared, "You meant evil against me, but God meant it for good" (Genesis 50:20). Joseph's story reminds us that even in the midst of suffering, God is working behind the scenes to bring about something far greater than we can see at the moment. David, too, faced rejection and peril, notably when he was anointed king but had to endure years of fleeing from King Saul, who saw him as a threat. David's faith in God's timing and his willingness to trust God's protection—such as when he faced Goliath—ultimately led to his rise to the throne. His story illustrates the reality that God's plan often unfolds in unexpected and challenging ways, but His hand is on us, guiding us toward His intended purpose.

Then, there's the story of Jesus, whose birth was marked by a king's fear and malice. King Herod's order to slaughter infants stemmed from a desire to prevent the rise of a new king who could threaten his own power. Yet, the evil actions of Herod could not thwart God's plan of salvation through Jesus. Jesus's life, death, and resurrection marked the ultimate victory over sin, death, and evil, securing redemption for humanity. His story shows that even in the face of opposition—whether from Herod or the forces of darkness—God's will cannot be undone. As for confronting our own "Herods," we all face challenges and obstacles in life, some of which are deeply rooted in the brokenness of the world. But the common thread among Joseph, David, and Jesus is that God does not leave us in our suffering; He uses it to fulfill a higher purpose. The realities of sin and hardship will always be a part of life, even for children, but in the midst of those challenges, God is at work, offering hope and the promise of His presence, just as He did for His faithful servants in Scripture. The stories of Joseph, Daniel, and Jesus offer powerful examples of enduring suffering, remaining faithful, and finding hope despite adversity.

During my time of living in the basement, where I spent many nights tossing shoes at the broken A/C to shew away the rats, I met the father of my children. I was 17, and he was 24. He came into my life like a whirlwind, full of energy and promises. He was from New York and painted this picture of a life that I had never experienced—one filled with excitement, love, and freedom. And honestly, it didn't take much to impress me, given that most of my childhood had been spent confined to my room when I wasn't in school. He took me everywhere. He bought me new clothes, took me on real dates, and for the first time in my life, I felt what it was like to be wanted. But the moment that truly captivated me was when he brought me home to meet his family. A family. A real family. I was in awe of them. They were bonded in a way I had never seen before. They laughed together, ate meals together, hugged one another, and stood united. They fought for each other, not against each other. It was a stark contrast to the chaos and isolation I had known growing up. I think I fell in love with them before I even felt love for him. For many years, I came to realize that it wasn't just him I was drawn to—it was the love and connection within his family that I so desperately craved.

They represented everything I had ever wanted but never had. They gave me a glimpse of what life could look like, and for someone who had lived in survival mode for so long, that was intoxicating. Now, I wish I could tell you that this family was perfect—that there were no issues, no dysfunction, no pain. But that would be a lie. Like any family, they faced their share of heartbreak, addiction, loss, struggles, and confrontations. The difference was that through it all, there was always love. They were far from perfect, but they remained connected, bound by something I hadn't experienced in my own upbringing. However, my ex-husband was a huge source of pain for his family. He battled addiction, struggled with mental health issues, and carried a darkness within himself that no one seemed able to penetrate. He was angry, lost, and destructive, and despite their love for him, not even his family could bring him out of the shadows. It wasn't long after we were together that

I experienced that darkness firsthand. It came in the form of a sharp, burning slap across my face during a heated argument, followed by a string of vile insults that shattered any illusion of the man I thought I knew. That night was just the beginning. The abuse became a regular part of my life—physical, verbal, and even sexual. I had traded one nightmare for another. It was a cruel twist of fate, but one I didn't immediately recognize as I tried to cling to the dream of the family I thought I was gaining. For every moment of love and warmth I felt from his family, there was an equal measure of pain and fear brought on by the man I had chosen to build a life with.

For the next 20 years, I lived in fear, chaos, and a darkness I didn't want to be in—but couldn't see my way out of. I had been beaten, verbally torn down, stolen from, cheated on, raped, and abandoned. And as much as I endured the pain, I found myself consumed by a new emotion: anger. Anger at him for everything he did, but mostly, anger at myself. How could I fall victim to abuse again? How could I not see the warning signs? How could I allow myself to endure this cycle once more? But the truth—the hard, painful truth—was that I stayed. I thought if I loved him enough, cared for him enough, and prayed hard enough, he would change. That he would see the good in me and in our family, and we would somehow overcome the destruction. I convinced myself that if I held on just a little longer, my family would become what I always dreamed it could be: whole, happy, and better. What I didn't want to admit—what I didn't even want to acknowledge—was that I wasn't staying out of hope. I stayed because of fear. Fear of being alone. Fear of failing my children. Fear that leaving would mean facing a world I didn't know how to navigate on my own. Fear that maybe I deserved it. Fear had built a cage around me, and I let it keep me there, mistaking survival for strength and endurance for love.

All I've heard my entire life is how strong I was, how brave I must have been to endure everything I did and somehow escape it. People marveled at my ability to survive, at my resilience in the face of so much pain and hardship. But what they didn't see—what I couldn't always put into words—was how broken I felt inside. They didn't see the nights I cried myself to sleep, feeling more like a shell of a person than someone brave or strong. They didn't see the doubt that consumed me, the shame that whispered that maybe I wasn't worth anything more than what I'd endured. They didn't see the weight of fear that still lingered long after I had escaped, or the anger I carried for allowing myself to stay in situations I knew I shouldn't have.

The truth is, survival didn't always feel like strength. It felt like desperation, like grasping at straws just to make it to the next day. It felt like holding my breath, hoping I wouldn't drown under the pressure of it all. And while I've learned to wear the title of "strong" with some measure of pride, I know now that strength isn't just about enduring. It's about healing, growing, and refusing to let the pain define who I am. That's the kind of strength I'm still learning to embrace. Fear, by its very definition, is debilitating. It creeps into the corners of our minds and wraps itself around our hearts, convincing us of lies that hold us captive.

I am convinced that the power we give fear is what chains us to the very things we long to escape. It keeps us in bondage—bondage to abuse, oppression, addiction, or anything else the enemy uses to trap us and keep us stuck in a cycle of despair. Fear kept me bound for years. Fear of being killed. Fear of being homeless. Fear that I would never know real love without abuse. Fear that I was not good enough—not as a wife, a sister, a friend, or a mother. And certainly not good enough to think that God would turn His ear to me, let alone deliver me from the hands of the enemy who had worked so diligently to keep me imprisoned. But here's the truth I've come to realize: The enemy didn't succeed because he was stronger or smarter than me. He succeeded because I gave him the power to succeed. I handed him the keys to my mind and heart when I allowed fear to dictate my actions, my thoughts, and my beliefs about myself. Fear is a liar, but it is only as powerful as the strength we give it. And for too long, I allowed it to reign over my life. But what I've learned is this: Fear can be defeated. Its chains can be broken. And the moment we choose to stop feeding it, stop believing its lies, and start trusting in the truth of who God says we are, fear begins to lose its grip.

My mother-in-law is so much more than that title can ever truly recognize. At the age of 17, I walked into her home as her son's girlfriend—a young girl who was homeless, beaten down, and utterly lost. When he introduced me to her, he didn't hold back about my situation. She could have hesitated or turned me away, but instead, she welcomed me with open arms. She gave me a home, but more importantly, she gave me a mother's love—a love I so desperately needed.

And most of all, she gave me Jesus. She wasn't just a woman of faith; she is a Godly woman.

The kind of woman who, the moment her eyes open and her feet hit the floor, is ready to intercede on behalf of her family, her friends, and even strangers. She is a prayer warrior in the truest sense. She and God? They're friends. They have a relationship so deep and so intimate that it's undeniable. I learned very early on that when she speaks, Heaven listens. Her faith is unwavering, her courage undeniable, and her relationship with God a living testimony to His goodness and power. From her, I learned about faith—real faith that stands firm even in the storms of life.

I learned about courage, the kind it takes to keep moving forward when life tries to knock you down. And I learned about the importance of a relationship with God, not just a belief in Him, but an active, living, breathing connection. She showed me what it means to conquer not through force, but through surrender—to fall to your knees in prayer and rise with the strength of God behind you. I've witnessed her cry out to God in prayer, night after night. I've heard her weep, plead, and intercede for her family, her loved ones, and anyone in need. And I've also seen how God honors those prayers. Time and time again, her faithfulness and her fasting brought breakthroughs that could only come from the hand of God. She taught me that prayer isn't just something you do in a moment of need—it's a lifestyle, a weapon, and a source of unshakable power. My mother-in-law gave me a home when I had none, but she gave me so much more than that. She gave me the foundation to build my faith, the courage to face life's battles, and the example of a woman whose life is a living testimony of God's grace. For that, I will forever be grateful.

Although I was being taught about faith and the power of God, my journey away from the Lie of Fear was far from walking fully in faith. I prayed. I read the Word. I went to church. But I didn't surrender. I didn't trust God—not really. I said I did. Every time I prayed, I told God I believed. But the truth was, I didn't. I kept trying to figure it all out by myself. I kept trying to stay in control when, in reality, I had no control at all.

Looking back, I often tell people it's like asking God to drive the car, but you refuse to get out of the driver's seat. You sit there with both hands gripping the steering wheel, your foot firmly on the gas, while God waits patiently in the passenger seat for you to realize that you don't actually know how to drive. You don't know where to go, when to stop, when to speed up, or how to avoid a collision. And when everything starts to spiral, you scream out, "God, help me!"—but you still don't let go of the wheel. That was me. I kept asking God to help, but I didn't really allow Him to do anything. I didn't give Him full control. I wanted Him to fix everything, but on my terms, in my timing. I thought if I just said the right words, if I just checked the boxes—pray, read, go to church—then somehow, everything would fall into place. But it doesn't work that way. Faith isn't just words. Faith without works is dead. The work of faith is surrender. It's letting go of the wheel, stepping out of the driver's seat, and letting God take control. It's trusting Him even when you don't understand the road ahead, even when it feels like you're heading straight into a storm. It's believing that His plan is better than yours, that His timing is perfect, and that He knows exactly where to take you—even when you have no clue. I wasn't there yet. I wasn't ready to surrender. I thought I could handle it, figure it out, and fix it all on my own. But the more I tried to control everything, the more I realized how much I was failing. I was trying to fight fear with my own strength, not realizing that the real victory could only come through faith—faith that isn't just spoken, but lived. Faith that lets God drive the car.

Faith that trusts Him completely, even when it feels impossible. I spent many years in turmoil. My ex-husband was addicted to crack and alcohol. He was mentally unstable, and I am convinced he was filled with many demonic spirits. I say this with certainty because, on several occasions, those spirits made themselves known. I can still see the distorted faces, the gleaming, unnatural eyes in the dark, and hear the chilling laughter in a voice I did not recognize—often after he had beaten me.

These weren't arguments that spiraled out of control. These were attacks born out of something far more sinister. I can recall nights waking to a pounding fist to my head because he dreamed I had been unfaithful. Nights where I sat frozen in fear as he poked me with kitchen knives, his snicker echoing through the room before he nonchalantly walked back to the bedroom to sleep. There were days he stood in the corner, screaming at something invisible, begging it to leave him alone. Then, he would turn to me and whisper in terror that "they" owned him and wouldn't let him go. There are countless memories like these, but just these moments alone are enough to haunt me for a lifetime.

The physical abuse, the mental torment, and the spiritual darkness were unbearable. Yet, somehow, I stayed. I prayed desperately, but I also got in God's way. I tried to fix him. I tried to save him. I thought it was my responsibility. I spent many nights walking the streets of Bushwick, Brooklyn, alone, trying to find him—trying to save him from death. Drug dealers were hunting him. Loan sharks were after him. And somehow, I believed that if I could just find him, I could save him. Of course, this was not my job. This was never my burden to carry. But I couldn't see that at the time. When I look back on those nights, wandering through the most dangerous parts of the city, I know it was only God's grace that kept me safe. I can imagine God shaking His head, watching me, saying, "This silly daughter of mine just doesn't get it!" If you know anything about Bushwick, Brooklyn, in the '80s and early '90s, you know how reckless it was for me to be out there alone at night. Yet I walked those streets, driven by a misguided sense of duty, blinded by fear and desperation. Those streets were no place for anyone, let alone a woman wandering alone. But somehow, I survived.

I wasn't ready to surrender, and I certainly wasn't ready to trust God fully, but even in my stubbornness, His grace covered me. It was a reckless grace, one I didn't deserve but one that held me through those dark, dangerous nights. What truly boggled my mind was that fear never stopped me from fighting for the people I loved. When it came to my children, my family, and my friends, I believed in the power of prayer. I stood on faith, interceding for them with a fierce determination. But when it came to me? I didn't have that same confidence. I couldn't find the strength to fight for myself the way I fought for others. Maybe it was because I had endured for so long. Maybe it was because I only knew abuse, disappointment, and pain. Or maybe it was because I kept looking at my circumstances with my natural eyes, unable to hope for something beyond the moment I was trapped in. My faith felt solid when it was for someone else, but when it came to believing God would deliver me, I hesitated. I doubted.

I was so tired. Tired of the life I was living. Tired of the marriage that kept me bound. Tired of my own mind and body betraying me. I wanted out—out of everything. I wanted freedom, but I didn't know how to be free. I had heard the words: "Give it to God." I had been told what freedom looked like in Him. But how could I give it all to God when trusting Him felt impossible? How could I trust that He wouldn't let me down when everyone else in my life had? I was used to disappointment. It had become my reality. So, why would God be any different? Why would He show up for me when no one else ever had? These thoughts haunted me, keeping me locked in a prison of doubt. I wanted freedom desperately, but I didn't know how to truly surrender and let go. I didn't know how to trust that God wouldn't let me fall. My fear wasn't just of my circumstances—it was of hoping for something better and being let down again.

CHAPTER 3

THE LIE OF FEAR

A WEAPON MADE POWERLESS

Through years of experience and reflection, I've come to understand that fear is both a powerful and powerless weapon wielded by the enemy. It's powerful because we, unknowingly, are the ones who give it its strength. Yet, it is also powerless because we hold the ability to strip it of that power. The choice lies within us. For so many years, fear held me in chains, dictating my actions, silencing my voice, and keeping me from stepping into the freedom God intended for me. God did not give us the spirit of fear. The words of 2 Timothy 1:7 became a lifeline: "For God has not given us a spirit of fear, but of power, love, and self-control." Think about that for a moment. The spirit of fear doesn't come from God—it's a tool of the enemy. What God has given us is far greater: power, love, and self-discipline. When I finally understood this truth, I realized that I didn't have to let fear dominate me any longer. I didn't have to live in bondage to it. I had, and still have, the power through God to silence fear, to bind its grip, and to cast it out. Now, don't get me wrong—this revelation didn't mean the journey to overcoming fear was easy. It isn't easy. Fear doesn't just walk away willingly; it fights back. But here's the beauty of it: We've already been equipped to win that fight. The spirit God has given us isn't timid; it's courageous. It doesn't cower; it conquers. With God's power, we can rebuke fear, render it powerless, and toss it over the cliff where it belongs. This isn't just wishful thinking—it's a divine promise. When we lean into the power, love, and self-discipline God has placed within us, fear has no choice but to bow. The journey to overcoming fear begins with the understanding that its strength comes only from the power we give it. Once we stop feeding it, it starves. Once we confront it with God's truth, it crumbles. And once we declare that we are no longer its captives, we begin to walk in the freedom God intended for us all along. Fear may knock at the door, but we don't have to let it in.

Living in the Chains of Fear

For over 20 years, I stayed in a marriage bound tightly by the chains of fear. Fear became my captor, whispering lies and threats into my ear, and I believed every single one. The enemy told me, "If you leave, he will find you. He will kill you. Your children will grow up without you." Fear convinced me that I'd be alone, that I'd crawl back, that leaving would bring more grief than staying. It played on my exhaustion, my doubt, and my desperation. The storm I was in was predictable—I knew its patterns, its intensity. It was chaos, but it was chaos I could anticipate. Someone once told me, "You get comfortable with the uncomfortable because you know what to expect." That was my life. I was comfortable in my discomfort because fear made the unknown seem so much worse than the pain I already endured. Fear kept me shackled to a mindset of mere survival. I wasn't living—I was just making it through each day, grateful I survived until the next. I couldn't dream, plan, or hope for something better because fear wouldn't let me look forward. It trapped me in the here and now, with no vision of a future beyond the storm. And oh, how I became accustomed to that storm. The winds of verbal abuse, the rains of physical pain, the thunder of isolation—these were constants in my life. I learned to weather them. But in my survival, I never sought out the calm. Fear told me it didn't exist. Fear told me this storm was all there was.

What I didn't realize was that while I was focusing on surviving the storm, I was allowing fear to block my view of the horizon. I didn't trust God to guide me to safety. I didn't believe there was calm on the other side of the chaos. Fear had me so blindfolded, I couldn't see that God was right there, waiting for me to take His hand and walk out of it. Fear thrives in darkness, in silence, in our inability to see forward. It thrives when we settle for less, believing the lies it feeds us. It took me years to see that the storm wasn't permanent—that God had calm waters waiting for me. I just had to trust Him enough to walk through the storm and leave fear behind.

As I sit here on Christmas Eve morning of 2024, I find myself reflecting on Christmases past. Christmas has always held a special place in my heart, my favorite of all holidays. But it's funny how, up until 2008, the season was often a tangled mixture of joy, sorrow, and fear. Fear, uninvited yet persistent, seemed to find its way into every holiday.

Or perhaps, deep down, I left the door open for it, giving it permission to sit at my table and feast on my peace. As a child, my mother shared the story of Jesus with me—the miraculous story of his birth to a virgin, his arrival in a humble manger, and his purpose as the Savior of the world. I didn't fully understand the power of that story then, but something about it resonated. It planted a small seed of hope in my heart. But growing up in a home shadowed by addiction, abuse, and relentless chaos, that hope felt distant. The reality of my life made the story of Jesus feel more like a fairy tale—a beautiful story but far removed from the world I knew. Yet, even in my doubt, there was something about that story that gave me a flicker of comfort. I held on to it, even if only faintly, as though it might one day prove itself real.

When I met my children's father, I desperately wanted Christmas to be different—a day of love, joy, and renewal. But instead, it became another day where fear took its place at the table. Every year, I woke up hoping, praying that this Christmas would be free from fear and disappointment. And every year, fear showed up, nourished by the familiar dysfunction of addiction and abuse. Most Christmases with him were unpredictable. On good mornings, my children would wake up to gifts under the tree, their smiles lighting up the room. But too often, they would wake to disappointment. I would lie to them, telling them a toy they had longed for was broken and had to be exchanged, knowing full well it had been sold the night before to feed their father's addiction. Christmas Eve and Christmas Day were battlegrounds, where my ex-husband's addiction clashed with my desperate attempts to salvage joy for my children. He would leave—sometimes in the middle of the night, sometimes before the day even began—taking gifts with him to pawn or sell. I would be left trying to piece together what remained, trying to shield my children from the reality of what was happening.

I feared Christmas because I knew what it would bring. The smiles I tried to create for my children always came with a heavy price—a price I paid in anxiety, disappointment, and heartbreak. Fear wasn't just a guest at my table; it was a constant presence, looming over the season that was supposed to bring peace and hope. But even in those darkest moments, I held on to a faint belief in the story my mother had shared with me—the story of the baby in the manger, the Savior of the world. It was a small ember of hope, barely visible amid the ashes of my circumstances, but it was there. And somehow, it was enough to keep me going.

As I sit here, memories flood my mind, a mix of sadness and gratitude. I think back to the countless times drug dealers banged on our door, demanding payment for what my ex-husband owed them. They came because he had "credited" drugs from them, leaving us in the aftermath of his choices. Those moments were filled with fear—fear of what they might do, fear of losing what little stability I tried to create for my children. But in the midst of that fear, I also felt a burning anger that pushed me to stand my ground. Looking at those men, I saw more than just individuals. I saw the very essence of the murderer, the thief, and the destroyer at work. These were people who played a role in tearing families apart, fueling addiction, and destroying the lives of those who sought the poison they sold.

They represented everything I despised—the audacity to profit off others' pain, to perpetuate a cycle of brokenness. And yet, in those moments, despite my fear, I stood firm and demanded they leave. I thought about the money I worked so hard to earn, money meant to provide for my children, slipping through my fingers and into theirs. I thought about the countless gifts, food, and clothes I carefully saved for and purchased, only to have them stolen from my children in exchange for drugs. It enraged me, and that anger gave me courage, or perhaps recklessness, to face them head-on. It's almost laughable to me now, the audacity I had to stand up to them. I remember going to their homes, walking through those dangerous doors, and standing toe-to-toe with them and their partners. I demanded what was rightfully mine—cars, money, belongings—whatever my ex-husband had traded away.

Looking back, I realize how foolish I was, how unaware of the real danger I put myself in. But now I see something else in those moments. It wasn't my anger or my courage that protected me. It wasn't even my sheer determination to reclaim what had been lost. It was God's grace. His grace covered me, shielded me, and carried me through. I imagine God watching me in those moments, shaking His head at my foolishness, thinking, *My daughter has no idea the peril she's placing herself in, but I will protect her anyway.* His grace, not my own strength, kept me alive, kept me standing. And for that, I am filled with gratitude. I didn't see it then, but I see it now: It was never my fight to win, but He kept me in the battle long enough to realize I didn't need to fight alone. Many will say I was foolish to stay.

Many will criticize me for allowing him to take from me and my children. But what many don't understand is that when you are in bondage—tied up and bound by the spirit of fear—you don't know how to be free. Fear doesn't just paralyze you; it blinds you, distorting your perception of reality until even the thought of freedom feels impossible. I tried everything I could think of to survive. I hid money, fought him physically, lied, and attempted to outsmart him at every turn. But leave? At that time in my life, leaving was nothing more than a distant fantasy. I couldn't even begin to imagine it as an option. I felt obligated to stay, convinced that leaving would mean breaking apart my family.

As dysfunctional and broken as it was, it was still mine. Leaving felt like a betrayal of the very idea of family, and worse, I believed it would lead to my death at his hands. I couldn't see hope in leaving. I couldn't see freedom. I only hoped that if I was good enough—if I prayed for him enough, supported him enough, loved him enough—he would stop. I believed that if I tried harder, he would see the love I had for him and choose us over his addiction. But that hope wasn't rooted in faith or truth; it was rooted in fear. The harsh truth is, I only saw survival. I had lived in chaos my entire life, so I didn't know how to recognize peace, let alone pursue it.

Fear whispered to me daily that this was as good as it was going to get, that staying alive and enduring the abuse was better than the unknowns of leaving. Fear had convinced me that gratitude for mere survival was enough to sustain me, even as it slowly and strategically worked to bring me to a mental and spiritual death. In hindsight, I see how fear played its hand. It wasn't just the fear of physical harm; it was the fear of the unknown, the fear of change, and the fear of failure. Fear is patient and calculated, and it feeds on your hope, replacing it with resignation. I thought I was holding on for love, for family, for faith—but really, I was just trying to keep fear at bay, not realizing I had given it dominion over my life. It took time, pain, and a lot of soul-searching to realize that freedom wasn't just an illusion. It was a choice. But in those dark days, fear had me convinced otherwise.

The abuse I endured at the hands of my ex was far from rational—not that abuse ever is—but this was something darker, more sinister, and beyond reason. Many people imagine abuse in a marriage stemming from arguments that spiral out of control or a partner's need for dominance. But what I experienced was more than that. It was unprovoked, erratic, and, at times, almost incomprehensible. I remember events that still haunt me to this day—moments that had no trigger, no justification, and no warning. One night, I was asleep, only to be jolted awake by a fist slamming into my head because he dreamed I was cheating on him. Another time, we were out to eat with our children.

What started as smiles and laughter quickly turned into seething anger, threatening words, and chaos, all in a matter of moments. It was as if I could see the devil himself sitting across from me at that table, using my ex as his vessel. That night ended in sheer humiliation, pain, and terror. My head throbbed from the repeated blows to my skull, and my mind raced as I drove frantically with my children in the backseat, desperate to find safety. I remember him abruptly leaving the vehicle in the middle of a highway exit, storming off into the night. My sons sat frozen in fear, asking me if I was okay and urging me to keep driving. We ended up sleeping for a few hours at a rest stop that night. My head pounded, my vision blurred—not just from tears but from the physical trauma I'd just endured. As I sit here writing this, that night comes back to me vividly. And my first thought is this: God's grace. Let me tell you why.

Years after I divorced this man, I began experiencing regular headaches. They became persistent enough that I finally saw a neurologist. After completing a series of tests, the doctor explained that I was dealing with migraines, likely triggered by hormonal changes as I approached menopause. But then he asked me something that stopped me in my tracks: "Have you ever been in an accident or experienced blunt trauma to your head?" Confused, I asked why. He explained that my brain scan showed scar tissue consistent with trauma—evidence of a significant impact to my skull. I sat there, stunned, as the memories flooded back. I thought of that night on the highway and countless others when I endured his violent outbursts. And then, amidst the pain and the memories, gratitude washed over me. The enemy's intent was clear. His goal was to destroy me—to take me out completely. But God's grace intervened. The same grace that protected me during those nights of terror, that kept me alive when all odds were against me, and that carried me forward even when I didn't know how to move. The enemy had a plan for my destruction, but God had a greater plan for my survival and redemption. That scar tissue, though a physical reminder of the abuse, is also a testament to the fact that I'm still here. I survived. Not because of my own strength, but because God's grace refused to let the enemy win.

As I sit here writing this book, I reflect on the pieces of my life I've shared with you so far—the moments of enduring physical, sexual, and mental abuse. But oh, let me tell you, there is so much more to this than what the eyes have seen or what the physical body has endured. Beyond the surface of my experiences lies a spiritual battle—a world unseen but deeply felt. I have encountered, seen, and even heard the enemy himself, or at least his soldiers, sent to torment me. My spiritual mother taught me so much about God, but she also taught me about the spirit world, about demonic forces, and how to view these battles through a spiritual lens. As my faith grew, so did my discernment. My spiritual eyes began to open, and with that growth came more intense attacks from the enemy. The more I sought God, the more determined the forces of darkness became to deter me. I remember one night vividly—a night when the veil between the natural and spiritual worlds seemed to lift. I was lying in bed with my two baby boys sleeping peacefully beside me. Their father was away at yet another rehab facility, and for the first time in a while, I thought I could rest in peace. But peace was the last thing I found. As I lay in the dark, my bed began to shake.

At first, I thought it must have been something simple, like the dog moving beneath it. Then came the buzzing—a persistent, irritating sound, like a fly buzzing near my ears. Annoyed, I jumped to my feet, turned on the light, and looked for the source. But the dog wasn't under the bed, and there was no fly in sight. I returned to bed, brushing it off as my imagination. But it wasn't my imagination. Each time I tried to sleep, the bed shook harder, and the buzzing grew louder. I couldn't explain it. My natural eyes saw nothing, but my spirit knew something was there. Then, in an instant, the shaking intensified, and I felt an invisible force grip my shoulders, holding me down and shaking me violently. My heart pounded, and fear swept over me as I realized this was no longer a natural annoyance but a spiritual attack. Terrified, I jumped out of bed and stayed awake, too afraid to close my eyes again. As soon as the sun rose, I ran to my spiritual mother and explained what had happened. She listened intently, her face calm but serious. Being the intercessor that she is, she didn't hesitate to take action.

She led me in prayer—fervent, commanding prayer that called on the power of God to bind the demonic forces that had invaded my home. With unwavering authority, she prayed, rebuked, and declared the power of Jesus over my life and my children. She taught me how to wield prayer as a weapon, how to take authority over the unseen, and how to demand that anything not of God leave my space. That night, I learned that while the enemy might come to shake us—both literally and spiritually—he cannot stand against the power of God. I also learned that prayer is not just a cry for help; it is a weapon. It is the armor that shields us, the sword that cuts through darkness, and the declaration of victory over forces that want to see us destroyed.

That experience stayed with me. It taught me that fear, though it tries to paralyze, cannot win when you stand in the authority God has given you. It also reminded me of the relentless grace and protection of God, who will never leave us defenseless in the face of spiritual battles. And through it all, my faith grew stronger, and the enemy's grip grew weaker. Not instant, but a process! As I grew in my prayer life and held on to the belief that somehow, my prayers would reach God's ears, the spiritual attacks intensified. It was as though the enemy became more desperate, refusing to let go of the grip he thought he had on my life. One night stands out vividly in my memory—a night that reminded me of the real battle I was facing, not just in the natural world but in the spiritual realm. I was lying in bed, pouring my heart out to God in prayer. I was asking Him for help, for strength, for a way out of the chaos that surrounded me. I was vulnerable, crying out to Him, and the enemy wasn't going to sit back and allow that without a fight.

As I prayed, I suddenly felt a force—hands around my throat, squeezing tightly, cutting off not only my breath but my very words of prayer. I was being strangled, not by something I could see, but by something I could feel. Fear surged through me, threatening to silence the prayer I was desperately trying to utter. In that terrifying moment, I remembered the teachings of my spiritual mother. She had told me about the power of prayer, about how it is not just words but a weapon. She had taught me to press through, even when fear seemed overwhelming. So, through the tears and the choking grip around my throat, I cried out to God. I declared His power over the enemy. I demanded the devil to flee in the name of Jesus. And then, the grip loosened. The air returned to my lungs. The darkness that had surrounded me lifted. I knew in that moment that God had heard me, that His power was greater than any force trying to hold me down. You would think that this experience would have been the turning point, that I had finally overcome fear. But fear still lingered.

It still resided in the corners of my mind and heart, waiting for opportunities to creep back in. While I was learning to believe in the power of prayer and beginning to use it as my weapon, I hadn't fully evicted fear from my life. I still held on to the steering wheel! The truth is, fear is persistent. It doesn't leave just because we've had a moment of victory. It tests us, waits for us to waver, and tries to reclaim the ground we've taken. I was learning to fight, but I hadn't yet learned to conquer. I still allowed fear to reside within me, a tenant I hadn't yet realized I had the authority to evict. What I didn't fully grasp at the time was that the battle wasn't just about prayer or belief; it was about surrender—complete and total surrender to God. I had to trust Him not just with my words but with my whole being. I had to stop holding on to the fear, stop letting it have a seat at the table, and start walking in the power, love, and sound mind that God had already given me.

This was the beginning of a journey—a journey to not just fight fear but to overcome it completely. And while I didn't know it then, God was already equipping me for the battles ahead, teaching me that His grace, His power, and His presence would always be greater than the fear that sought to hold me captive. There are countless events from my childhood and adult life that I could recount. I could share every detail, paint every painful picture, and dive deep into the darkness of abuse I endured. But that's not why I'm sharing this with you. My goal isn't to lead you down a dark hole of abuse—physical, emotional, and sexual.

The truth is, many children and women have endured the same horrors, and many have faced abuse that was far worse than mine. The bruises scattered across my body, some lingering for weeks before they faded, told only part of the story. The broken bones, the deep lacerations—each one a painful reminder of the battles I had endured. But as agonizing as they were to see and feel, they were nothing compared to the invisible wounds etched into my soul. The damage to my self-worth, the shattering of my pride, and the erosion of my faith cut deeper than any physical injury ever could. These wounds didn't fade with time; they lived beneath my skin, reminding me every day of the fear, the doubt, and the pain that refused to let go. My stepfather's wooden sticks, belt buckles, and clenched fists left their mark on my skin, but their pain was fleeting—trivial compared to the wounds they carved into my spirit. The sting of each blow faded, yet the scars of violation, betrayal, abandonment, and the aching absence of love lingered long after.

My ex-husband's fists and feet battered my body, leaving behind broken bones, knots, bruises, cuts, and scars—painful reminders of his power and my helplessness. But even those were nothing compared to the torment he inflicted on my soul. The forced invasion of my body was an unspeakable cruelty, yet the deepest wounds were not the ones that bled. It was the hopelessness that consumed me, the fear that chained me, and the slow, agonizing loss of the woman I once was. His abuse didn't just hurt me—it tried to erase me. You see, I endured broken bones, sprained wrists and ankles, and legs so swollen from the blows that I could barely stand. My ribs ached from the force of his rage, my fingers were bound in splints, and even my brain carried the scars of his violence. But none of it—none of the physical pain, the bruises, or the wounds—could compare to the relentless beating that fear inflicted on me. Fear was the real abuser. It crushed me in ways no fist ever could, chaining me to silence, stripping me of my worth, and suffocating every ounce of hope. The bruises eventually faded, the bones mended, but fear remained—deep, paralyzing, and unrelenting. And that was the wound that hurt the most. I am not unique in my suffering. But I am unique in my journey. In 2008, I hit a wall. I was tired—mentally, physically, emotionally tired.

My spirit felt crushed under the weight of years of pain and hopelessness. I had fought hard against the whispers of suicide, silenced the urge to let myself completely fall apart, and rejected the idea of seeking help through hospitalization. I didn't make those choices for myself—I made them for my sons. You see, I knew what it felt like to be abandoned by the very people who were supposed to love me, protect me, and fight for me. I knew the ache of being left behind, and I couldn't allow my sons to feel that same pain. No matter how hopeless I felt, no matter how much I wanted to give up, I couldn't throw in the towel because I knew they needed me. Even on the hardest days, when I felt like I had no fight left, I would look at my sons and find a reason to keep going. They became my anchor, my light in the darkness. I absolutely believe that God gave them to me for this very purpose. And of course, His purpose for them as well. They were my reason to wake up every morning and decide that another day was worth surviving. When I reflect on those years, I often find myself thanking God for my boys.

Without them, I don't know where I would be. They reminded me that even in the midst of my suffering, I had something—someone—worth fighting for. They kept me grounded when I felt like I was losing my mind, gave me hope when all I could see was despair, and reminded me that my story wasn't over yet. God knew I needed them, just as He knew they needed me. And in many ways, they saved my life as much as I saved theirs. Together, we survived those dark days, and because of them, I began to see the glimmer of light at the end of the tunnel. They were my lifeline, and I will forever be grateful for the strength they unknowingly gave me to keep going.

The year 2008 was a turning point for me. It was the year I took my first leap of faith—a step toward reclaiming my life and breaking free from the chains that had bound me for so long. My ex-husband was in and out of jail, in and out of rehab, and as if that wasn't enough, he began seeing another woman. This time, he was bold about it, flaunting it as if to humiliate me. His anger toward me grew, fueled by the changes he saw in me—changes that threatened him. You see, I had decided to go back to school. I wanted to better myself, not just for me, but for my children. I wanted to be an example of what perseverance and achievement looked like.

I enrolled in online classes at the University of Phoenix to pursue a degree in psychology. It was a small step, but for me, it was monumental. But he hated it. Every day, as I sat at the computer working on my assignments, he tormented me. Random phone calls filled with threats to take my life, fights over imagined slights or fabricated scenarios—all designed to break me. He would accuse me of thinking I was better than him, of trying to leave him behind. His insecurity turned into rage, and his rage turned into a weapon he wielded against me. There were so many times I wanted to quit. The constant harassment, the physical and verbal abuse, the sheer exhaustion of living in survival mode—it all felt unbearable. I took breaks from my studies not because I wanted to but because I had to. I needed to regain my strength, to find a way to keep moving forward. And every time I wanted to give up, I looked at my sons. Their faces reminded me why I couldn't quit, why I had to press on. I stopped sleeping in my bed at night, too afraid of what might happen if he came home drunk and angry. He had threatened to slice my throat in front of our children, and those words haunted me. Sleep felt like a luxury I couldn't afford. Most nights, I sat in the living room, staring at the door, listening for his footsteps. Anxiety was my constant companion, and fear controlled my every move.

My days were an endless cycle of work, school, picking him up from wherever he had passed out drunk, enduring his fists and his words, and then watching the door until I fell into a restless sleep. I was exhausted—physically, mentally, emotionally. And I was angry. I was angry at myself for staying, angry at him for destroying what little peace I had, and most of all, angry at God. I had prayed so many times, begged God to save me from this nightmare, but nothing seemed to change. I felt abandoned by the very One I had placed my hope in. I couldn't smile anymore, couldn't fix one more problem, couldn't battle one more drug dealer or make one more excuse to those who asked if I was okay. I was done. In that moment, I hit rock bottom. But what I didn't realize was that rock bottom wasn't the end—it was the foundation where God was preparing me to rebuild. My journey wasn't over yet, but in that dark, desperate place, a spark of determination began to flicker. I didn't know it then, but that spark would one day grow into a flame that would light the path to my freedom. In the summer of that year, something shifted in my life.

My ex-husband was incarcerated for 90 days, and for the first time in years, I felt the faintest glimmer of relief. Around the same time, I agreed to let my sons spend the entire summer with their grandmother—a decision that was unusual for me, as I typically didn't allow them to be away for more than a few weeks. But this summer was different. This summer, I needed to breathe. I needed space. I needed a break from the constant chaos that had consumed my life for so long. Even though I still had to work, knowing he was behind bars and my children were safe and cared for gave me a sense of calm I hadn't experienced in years. It was in this space, this moment of reprieve, that something extraordinary happened. I yelled at God.

Every day, I fell to my face, tears pouring uncontrollably, and I screamed. I screamed at God, I cried, and I told Him exactly how I felt. I didn't hold back. I told Him I was angry, that I felt abandoned, that I couldn't believe anymore. I shouted that He had left me alone to endure years of torment, and I demanded answers. I poured out every ounce of pain, every frustration, and every hopeless thought. But something unexpected happened in the midst of my despair. As I lay there on the floor, face pressed against the ground, my screaming and sobbing began to shift. The intensity of my anger softened, and my cries turned into something deeper—something I didn't even realize I needed. My yelling became my surrender. For the first time in my life, I truly surrendered. You see, all those years of surviving, of praying for God to help me, I had never really allowed Him to. I prayed, sure—but they were hollow words with no true faith behind them. I prayed and then tried to handle everything myself. I prayed but still clung to the illusion of control. I didn't pray and truly give my burdens to God. I prayed while keeping my hands on the steering wheel of my life, trying to drive even when I didn't know where I was going. The truth is, I wasn't even the one driving. Fear was the driver, and I had willingly handed over the keys.

Every time I prayed but didn't believe in my heart that God would deliver me, I fueled Fear. I gave it power, and it kept me captive. I thought I was praying, but in reality, I was holding on to my chains. That summer, on the floor of my brokenness, I finally let go. I stopped yelling long enough to hear God whisper, "I'm here. I've always been here. But now, you've let me in." That was the moment I began to understand what it meant to have faith—not just to say I believed, but to live like I believed. It wasn't an instant transformation, but it was a beginning. A crack in the wall I had built around my heart. That summer, I gave God the keys. And while Fear still tried to ride along, it no longer had control of the wheel.

Now, I wish I could say that this was the end of my bondage, but it wasn't. This was just the beginning of me letting go and truly giving it to God. Over the next 90 days, I was being transformed, yes, but this wasn't the final chapter—it was the first step in the direction God wanted me to walk. When my children returned home and my ex-husband was released from prison, the familiar anxiety crept in. Knowing he was free felt like preparing for another round of chaos. But something was different this time. This time, I was ready—not ready to bow down and submit as I had so many times before, but ready to stand up and fight back. And this time, I wasn't relying on my own strength. I was relying on God to deliver me from the chains the enemy had wrapped around my feet. The day he was released from prison, he didn't come home. Instead, he spent the first three days with his mistress.

What's ironic is that while I was angry he didn't come home to see his sons, I was also relieved. I no longer loved him. I no longer wanted this marriage or the perfect family picture I had clung to in my mind. That image was shattered long ago. I wanted out. When he finally came home, I was at work. He called and asked me to come back so we could talk. When I arrived, he met me with words of promise—promises to be different, to change. Then, he extended his hand and offered me a gold chain with a cross attached to it. Ironic, isn't it? That he would offer me a cross, yet he was the carrier of every demonic force that had been trying to destroy me for years. That gesture sent me into a rage. In that moment, every memory of his betrayal, his violence, and his destruction flashed through my mind like a picture show. I found myself throwing anything within reach, hitting him with whatever I could grab. I'm not proud of my actions, and I'm not justifying them. Violence is never the answer. But that day, I felt the weight of years of pain rise to the surface. That day, I was no longer going to be his victim.

My spiritual mother was on the phone with me during this moment because he had called her and pleaded with her to talk to me so I would calm down and stop attacking him. Her voice was soft and calm as she begged me to stop. She said she understood my anger but pleaded with me not to hurt her son. It was her quiet, gentle words that calmed the storm inside me. He fled from the home, but I knew he would return. And when he did, I knew he would come back with a plan to hurt me. When he returned, his anger boiled over. He threw me up against the wall, his hands tightening around my neck. But what he didn't know was that I was prepared. I held tightly to a can of mace, and in that moment, I sprayed it into his eyes until he fell to the ground screaming. And yet, even then, I felt compassion. I dragged him to the sink, turned on the water, and rinsed his eyes. Then, I walked away.

When my sons came home, they saw the aftermath—broken glass everywhere, holes in the walls from the objects I had thrown. They screamed my name in fear, worried that I was hurt. But that day, I was okay. I was more than okay. I was not in a state of fear but anger. I assured them I was fine, told them to care for their father, and then I returned to work. That day, something shifted in me. I didn't have all the answers, but I knew I couldn't go back to what was. I didn't just want freedom—I was ready to fight for it.

What is fear? Fear is defined as an unpleasant emotion triggered by the belief that someone or something is dangerous, likely to cause pain, or presents a threat. It is a reaction that often immobilizes, controls, and dictates how we navigate our lives. Fear, in its simplest form, can shield us from danger, but when allowed to grow unchecked, it becomes a prison, holding us captive to its will. For much of my life, fear was not just an emotion—it was a dictator, a constant presence that whispered lies into my ear. It told me that danger was always around the corner, that I was powerless to escape it, and that any attempt to break free would bring consequences far worse than the pain I already endured. Fear became my lens, the filter through which I viewed every decision, relationship, and hope for the future. In a biblical sense, the word "fear" holds dual meanings. It can refer to the emotional response of dread and terror, or it can signify reverence and awe, particularly toward God. For me, fear in its most destructive form dominated my life. It wasn't the kind of fear that inspires reverence or leads to wisdom as described in Proverbs 9:10, "The fear of the Lord is the beginning of wisdom."

Instead, it was the crippling kind of fear that kept me chained—fear of the unknown, fear of harm, fear of failure, and fear of being abandoned. Looking back, I see how fear seeped into every crevice of my life. It was there in the abusive relationships I endured, whispering that leaving would be worse than staying. It convinced me that I was powerless, that no one could save me, and that trying to change my circumstances would only lead to greater suffering. It was fear that told me I wasn't good enough—that I wasn't a good enough wife, mother, daughter, or even a believer in God. Fear distorted my understanding of God's role in my life. I prayed, but my prayers were hollow, my faith weak. I allowed fear to be the driver, and though I often cried out for God's help, I wasn't willing to let go of the wheel. I didn't understand that surrendering to God required me to rebuke fear, to take back the power I had unknowingly given it.

The Weight of Fear's Power

Fear was not rational. It didn't wait for evidence or logic; it simply controlled. I feared leaving abusive situations because I believed the lies fear told me: "You'll never survive if you leave,if you ask for help. You'll lose everything, even your children." It's ironic because I was already losing so much by staying—my sense of self, my joy, my peace, and my faith in God's promises. Fear thrives on silence and isolation. It kept me from sharing my struggles, from reaching out for help, and from truly believing that I deserved a life free of torment. It made me settle for survival rather than seek freedom. What I didn't understand for so long is that fear's power is an illusion. It is only as strong as the power we give it. The Bible reminds us in 2 Timothy 1:7: "For God has not given us a spirit of fear, but of power, love, and self-control." I began to realize that fear was never meant to be my ruler; instead, God had given me the tools to fight it. Taking back the power from fear was not easy, and it didn't happen overnight. It required me to surrender, to trust God fully, and to believe in His promises even when my circumstances suggested otherwise. But once I began to lean into faith and step away from fear, I started to see the cracks in fear's hold over me.

Many years before I finally left in 2008, my spiritual mother called me into her bedroom. She had been in deep prayer, and God had given her a specific scripture to share with me: Isaiah 43:1–8. She read the words aloud to me with such conviction and tenderness, and for the first time in what felt like forever, I felt a spark of hope. God knew what to say to me and the right time to say it. The Scripture spoke directly to my soul: "But now, this is what the Lord says—He who created you, Jacob, He who formed you, Israel: 'Do not fear, for I have redeemed you; I have summoned you by name; you are mine.'" It was as if God Himself was speaking to me, reminding me that I belonged to Him, that He had not forgotten me, and that He had already claimed victory over the darkness that surrounded me. It gave me a sliver of reassurance that even though it seemed like He wasn't speaking to me in my darkest moments and wasn't actively delivering me from my circumstances, He was still there. His presence was real, even in my silence, even in my pain. I held on to those words, repeating them to myself whenever I felt like I couldn't go on. Isaiah 43 reminded me that God promised to walk with me through the waters so I wouldn't drown and through the fire so I wouldn't be burned.

At the time, I didn't fully understand how these promises would manifest in my life, but I clung to the possibility that they would. Looking back now, I realize how significant that moment was. My spiritual mother's obedience to share God's word with me planted a seed of hope. That Scripture became a lifeline, a reminder that even though I was waiting for my deliverance, I was not abandoned. God was there all along, preparing me for the moment when I would finally surrender and trust Him to lead me out of the storm.

I have come to understand that fear is one of the most powerful weapons the enemy uses to hold us captive and in bondage. Fear has the ability to control our thoughts, influence our actions, and paralyze our progress. When we give in to fear, we often find ourselves making impulsive decisions that can lead to irreversible consequences, or we become stagnant—frozen in place, unable to move forward because we've been completely debilitated by its grip. Throughout history and even in modern media, we see countless examples of horrific actions taken by individuals. While these actions are often attributed to emotions like jealousy, anger, or greed, I truly believe that at the root of so many of these decisions lies fear. Fear of not having enough. Fear of not being enough. Fear of not measuring up to others. Fear of being overlooked or underestimated. Fear of failure, rejection, or even success. When fear takes hold, it creates a reaction in us—one that can either shut us down entirely or ignite destructive behaviors. Fear pushes people to say or do things that are harmful, hurtful, and even dangerous. It clouds our judgment, weakens our resolve, and causes us to live from a place of insecurity and scarcity rather than faith and abundance.

Understanding fear in this way allows us to recognize its destructive potential, not just in our own lives but in the world around us. When we allow fear to dictate our actions, we are no longer walking in the truth of who we are called to be. It is only when we confront fear head-on, standing firm in faith and truth, that we can break free from its chains and step into the fullness of what God has for us. Fear may be a weapon, but it is a weapon we have the power to disarm. Let me make one thing perfectly clear: Fear only has the power you give it. I spent most of my life unknowingly fueling it, handing it the ammunition it needed to keep shooting me down and keeping me captive. I believed the lies it whispered, and in doing so, I gave it authority over my thoughts, actions, and decisions. But here's the truth—fear is powerless without our consent. And let's not forget this fundamental truth: The devil himself has no power over us. God has already claimed victory.

The enemy only holds power if we hand it to him—if we believe his lies, submit to his manipulations, and give him space to operate in our lives. His weapons, including fear, are ultimately powerless in the face of God's truth and authority. When we start to see fear for what it truly is—a lie designed to distract and derail us—we can begin to reclaim the power that belongs to us through God. We can stand firm, knowing that we are more than conquerors through Christ. Fear may try to deceive us, but it cannot defeat us unless we allow it to. And when we stop feeding fear, it loses its grip, and we are free to walk in the victory God has already given us.

The day I decided to leave my ex-husband was anything but easy. The anxiety was suffocating as I grabbed the suitcases I had hidden for my sons, loading them into the car with trembling hands. A voice in my head screamed that I was making a grave mistake—that he would find me, and that leaving with his children would cost me my life. Fear was relentless, whispering every worst-case scenario imaginable. But despite the weight of that fear, I pushed through. I told myself, *You cannot go back. You will not go back.* Believe me, I was terrified. I had reached out to a friend who lived in the next county, someone he had no knowledge of and no connection to. Her home became a safe haven, a place he couldn't track down—or so I told myself.

Yet, for the first two months of what became a three-month stay, I found myself constantly looking out the window, scanning every passing car, every unfamiliar face, waiting for the moment he would find us. I barely slept. Peace felt foreign to me, and I struggled to accept it. For so long, my life had been a constant cycle of chaos, and my mind had learned to always be on high alert. Letting my guard down, even for a moment, felt like a risk I couldn't afford to take. I was so conditioned to brace for the worst that I didn't know how to embrace the calmness of my friend's home. It was a daily battle, but one I had to face—because staying in fear wasn't living, and I was determined to build a life of freedom, not survival. Sleep didn't come easy for me. In fact, it never had. When I think about it, I realize that I spent most of my childhood and all of my married life sleeping with one eye open, always anticipating the next storm. And then there was the grief. You might ask, "What on earth were you grieving?

Grief is about loss, right? Surely, you should have been ecstatic to finally be free from this man." But what many don't understand is that grief isn't always about the loss of a person—it's also about the loss of time. I grieved the time. 20 years of my life, gone—years I could never give back to myself. I was angry, not just at him but at myself, for waiting so long, for enduring so much, for losing so much of my youth to pain and fear. I grieved the years I spent paralyzed by the lie of fear, unable to take the steps I had finally taken to free myself. I grieved for my children, for the broken home they now had to face as their reality. I grieved for the father they never truly had—the one I had prayed and hoped he would become but never was. I grieved for pulling them away from the familiarity of their home and the friendships they had built, uprooting their lives in search of safety. These emotions were overwhelming. They weighed heavily on me, sometimes so much that I felt like I couldn't breathe. So I shared it all with God. I laid it bare before Him, asking for peace and comfort because I knew I couldn't handle it alone. It was too much. And even in my grief, I knew He was the only one who could carry the weight I couldn't bear. Even though I was terrified of the unknown, I knew I had to push through. I filed for a restraining order with the courts, knowing it was the next necessary step. My ex continued to call and leave threatening messages, keeping me in a constant state of anxiety.

Then, something happened that I firmly believe was God's intervention. He violated the restraining order placed on him by his mistress—yes, she had one, too, as a result of him blaming her for my leaving and physically abusing her. This violation landed him back in jail. I used this time as an opportunity to gather all of my possessions and place them in storage. I prayed continuously for God to keep me moving forward and to help me resist the temptation to look back.

The day of my hearing, he was brought into the courtroom in handcuffs and ankle chains. The flood of emotions I experienced was overwhelming. I felt relief—finally, he was restrained, and I was safe, even if only temporarily. I felt like he deserved his current situation, a direct result of his actions. But then, I also felt sadness. Crazy, right? Sadness for the life he had chosen, for the bondage the devil had on him. What surprised me most was the empathy I felt.

Empathy for the woman he had chosen to commit adultery with, who was also in the courtroom that day for her hearing—same judge, same courtroom, same time. I felt sorry for her, knowing she was being confronted with the painful truth of who he really was. But among all these emotions, the one that stood out the most was release. For the first time, I felt free from the chains of fear that had bound me for so long. It was as though a weight had been lifted, and I could finally begin to breathe again. It wasn't just about him being in jail; it was about me stepping into a new chapter, one where I could walk forward without the constant shadow of his control looming over me. This was my moment of release.

Before my stepfather died, he asked for my forgiveness—and I freely gave it. Forgiving him didn't mean welcoming him back into my life or forgetting the pain he caused, but it was something I needed to do for my own peace. Not long after that, he passed away. Many people throughout my life have questioned my decision to forgive him. How can you forgive someone who molested you, beat you, deprived you of a normal childhood? Someone who took everything—your innocence, your self-worth, your peace? The answer is simple: I didn't forgive him for his sake; I forgave him for mine. Unforgiveness, I've learned, is like an open wound that refuses to heal. It festers, infecting your heart and mind until it creates a bitterness and hardness that affects every part of your life. Was I going to give his actions that kind of power over me? Absolutely not.

I chose to forgive so I could move forward without the weight of what he had done holding me back. I wanted to be free to love, free to trust, and free to give kindness to those I meet. Carrying the burden of anger and hatred would have only built walls around my heart, walls that would keep me from experiencing the fullness of life and relationships. Forgiveness doesn't erase what happened, nor does it excuse his actions. But it allowed me to reclaim my power and live without the chains of bitterness dragging me down. Forgiving him was a choice I made not to let his darkness define my life. It was a choice for freedom, for healing, and for the ability to keep my heart open to the beauty of life.

What Is Forgiveness?

At its core, forgiveness is the act of releasing anger, resentment, or the desire for retribution toward someone who has wronged us. It means choosing to "let go" of the offense, flaw, or mistake, and it is as much a gift to ourselves as it is to the person we forgive. Forgiveness doesn't mean condoning the wrong or forgetting what happened; it means deciding not to let the hurt have power over our lives anymore.

How Does God's Word Define Forgiveness?

According to the Bible, forgiveness is God's promise not to count our sins against us. It is rooted in His love and mercy, and it's through Jesus Christ that we experience this transformative gift. Forgiveness from God requires us to repent—turn away from our old lives of sin—and put our faith in Jesus Christ.

Letting Go

The literal meaning of forgiveness in the Bible is "to let go." It signifies releasing the offense, just as God releases our sins when we come to Him in faith. A powerful aspect of biblical forgiveness is that it is not conditional on the other person's actions. It stems from a willingness to extend grace and emulate God's forgiveness toward us.

The Role of Forgiveness in Our Lives

One condition for receiving God's forgiveness is our willingness to forgive others. As Jesus taught in Matthew 6:14–15: "For if you forgive other people when they sin against you, your Heavenly Father will also forgive you. But if you do not forgive others their sins, your Father will not forgive your sins." Forgiveness is not just an act of obedience to God; it's a pathway to healing and freedom. Holding on to anger or resentment keeps us in bondage, but forgiveness liberates us to live with peace and joy. In forgiving others, we reflect God's heart and His love for humanity. It allows us to live free of the bitterness and pain that unforgiveness can create, fostering relationships that are rooted in grace and compassion.

Forgiveness Is a Journey

Forgiving someone doesn't always happen overnight. It is often a process that requires God's help, especially in situations of deep hurt or betrayal. But through prayer and reliance on Him, forgiveness becomes possible—and with it comes peace that surpasses understanding. Choosing forgiveness means choosing to let go of the weight of anger and bitterness, and trusting God to bring healing, justice, and restoration. Now, listen—forgiveness didn't always come so easily for me.

My ex-husband was someone I couldn't bring myself to forgive until just a few years ago. It took many years to let go of the anger and hurt I carried so deeply within me. The wounds he left—both physical and emotional—were not just scars on my body and mind, but chains around my heart. What I came to understand, though, was that the unforgiveness I held on to wasn't hurting him—it was hurting me. It kept me in a constant state of fear and anxiety, even long after I had physically left that chapter of my life behind. Whenever I heard his voice or had to be in the same space as him for events involving our sons or family, the weight of those memories would flood back. I wasn't just afraid of him; I was still living in the shadows of the past, carrying the remnants of pain that he had inflicted on me.

The fear wasn't about the present—it was tied to the hold I allowed the past to have over me. And that hold remained because I refused to release it through forgiveness. When I finally chose to let go, I realized that forgiving him wasn't about excusing what he did or forgetting the pain he caused. It was about freeing myself from the burden of anger, resentment, and fear that I carried for so long. It was about reclaiming my peace and stepping into the fullness of the life God intended for me. Forgiveness became my way of breaking the chains—finally and fully—and walking in the freedom I had been searching for all along.

The Power of Forgiveness

Forgiveness is more than just a word or an act—it is a decision. A decision to release, to heal, and to walk in the grace that God so freely gives to us. It is saying, "No matter the offense, I choose to forgive the offender." Just as God extends His forgiveness to us despite our shortcomings, we are called to do the same. Forgiveness carries power—a power that unleashes love and grace not only upon us but also upon those we choose to forgive. It is not about excusing wrongs or pretending pain never existed. Instead, it is about freeing ourselves from the weight of resentment and opening the door for God's peace to reign in our hearts. But did you know that forgiveness has the power to shut down fear? When we hold on to unforgiveness, we carry anger, bitterness, and hurt like a heavy burden. These emotions fuel anxiety, creating a cycle of pain that feeds fear. But when we choose to forgive, we release that weight. We strip fear of its power by letting go of the very emotions that sustain it.

"Why would I ever give them forgiveness? Isn't that giving them an out? Doesn't that somehow justify their actions? Doesn't that give them a free pass?"

Absolutely not! Forgiveness wasn't about them—for me, it was about me. I needed to forgive so I could live. I needed to forgive so I could be free. I needed to forgive so I could be stronger, so I could continue to love, so I could be healthy in my mind and in my thoughts. I needed to forgive so I, too, could be forgiven. Forgiveness gave me relief—relief from the unbearable weight I had carried for so long. In my forgiveness, I gave it to God. In my forgiveness, I gave them to God. And when I did, I asked God to forgive them, to free them, to deliver them, to do a new thing in them. Forgiveness shut up the fear that was attached to my pain. Let me be clear: Forgiveness is not about accepting what someone has done to you. It is not about letting them back into your life. It is about not allowing the enemy to have power over you—to dictate how you think, how you move, how or if you will love. Forgiveness allowed me to exhale and move forward. So, today, I encourage you—release the weight. Let go of the fear. Walk in freedom. Because when we forgive, we don't just release others—we release ourselves.

After filing for and being granted my divorce in 2009, I thought I was finally free. I mean, after all, I left the abuse and the abuser. I had my own apartment with my sons, a decent job that paid the bills, and a newfound sense of independence. I was good, right? Wrong. What I didn't realize then was that freedom isn't just about leaving a situation or a person; it's about breaking the chains they left behind. Fear still had a place at my table. No, I was no longer being beaten up or beaten down physically, but emotionally and mentally, I was still very much a prisoner.

Doubt, feelings of inadequacy, and a crippling lack of self-worth lingered like uninvited guests in my life. I was no longer living in the storm, but the storm had taken up residence within me. I thought I could move on—I dated a few times and even entered a four-year relationship after my divorce. But fear whispered constantly in my ear, telling me I couldn't do better, I couldn't be loved better, that I wasn't pretty enough, smart enough, or worthy enough to deserve more. It wasn't just fear of others; it was fear of myself, of my decisions, of my future. This fear kept me bound. I saw red flags in every man I involved myself with, yet I would either run away too fast or, just like before, stay and try to make it work, even when I knew it wasn't right.

My anxiety and depression clung to me like old, tattered clothing I didn't know how to shed. I continued to feel everything I felt before—unworthiness, hopelessness, exhaustion—but most importantly, I continued to push God to the passenger seat. Even after everything, I was still trying to drive my own life, holding tightly to the wheel, navigating through my mess, and pretending like I had any idea where I was going. But the truth was, I had no clue. I was trying to move forward with the same old baggage in the trunk, too scared to unpack it and too stubborn to let God take the wheel. My idea of freedom had been so small and so shallow—just getting out of the situation I was in—but real freedom required so much more. It required surrender. And I wasn't ready for that yet. Well, let me correct that—I was ready, but I didn't know how to be ready. What exactly does being ready look like? I didn't know. I knew I wanted more for my life. I knew I was tired of the chains, tired of merely surviving. I was ready to live fully free, but the question was, how? How do you step into freedom when you've lived so long in bondage? On the surface, I was finally achieving external goals. I had completed my master's degree, a milestone that once felt like an impossible dream. I had landed a great job, moved into a nicer apartment, and upgraded to a better car. My sons were thriving and finding their paths, and from the outside, my life looked like it was all coming together. But the truth? My internal self was still the same. I carried the same struggles in my mind and the same brokenness in my heart.

The doubts, the insecurities, and the relentless whispers of unworthiness were as present as ever. I was still fighting the same battles, only now they were quieter, subtler—hidden behind the facade of achievement and success. Every day, I moved through life with a smile on my face, presenting the image of someone who had it all together. But beneath the surface, I felt like I was just going through the motions, still chained to the past, still struggling to believe that I could truly break free. The hardest part was realizing that all the external accomplishments couldn't heal the internal wounds. I had achieved so much, but those achievements couldn't fill the emptiness I felt inside. Freedom wasn't about a better car, a better job, or a nicer apartment. It was about breaking free from the lies I had believed about myself for so long, the lies that told me I wasn't enough, that I didn't deserve peace, that I couldn't be whole. I had done everything I thought I was supposed to do to build a better life, but what I hadn't done was the hard, painful work of letting go—of surrendering my heart and my mind to God completely. I thought I had, but I hadn't. And until I did, I knew I would never truly live the free, abundant life I was so desperately seeking.

A valuable moment in my journey began with fear—a fear that had long been a weapon against me. You might wonder, how could fear possibly be valuable if it's the very thing that kept me bound? Allow me to explain. I met my husband, Michael, in 2015, and we married six months later. That's another incredible story of God's work, but I'll save that for another time. Michael is a strong man, fiercely protective of me and our family. From the beginning, I felt secure with him, knowing that he would do whatever it took to protect me from harm. Naturally, you'd think that with Michael by my side, I'd never feel fear again, especially in the presence of my ex-husband. But that wasn't the case.

The day of my grandson's christening started with anxiety. I woke up knowing my ex-husband would be there. Not only would he be present, but as grandparents, we'd have to stand together on the pulpit while my grandson was being dedicated to God. The thought filled me with dread. As the time to leave for church drew near, my anxiety intensified. My hands trembled, my breathing grew shallow, and my mood darkened. When I shared my feelings with Michael, he didn't understand at first. He reassured me that I was safe, that no one could ever hurt me again with him by my side. Rationally, I knew he was right. Nothing was going to happen. But fear doesn't operate rationally, and my mind was flooded with what-ifs. Standing on the pulpit was almost unbearable.

My legs felt weak, and each breath seemed like a struggle. All I wanted to do was run. When the dedication was over, my son helped me down the steps, and I clung to my husband, pleading with him to take me home. Michael was angry—not at me, but at the power my ex-husband still seemed to hold over me. His frustration was a mirror, reflecting the truth I hadn't fully faced. I realized in that moment that I was still allowing fear to control me. I was annoyed with myself for letting it taint such a precious day, but the experience opened my eyes to something deeper: I wasn't fully delivered. It wasn't that God hadn't delivered me—He had. But I hadn't stood firmly on that deliverance. I had left the door cracked for fear to linger because I hadn't fully trusted God's promise. Did I truly believe that I had nothing to fear? The answer was no. Fear had stayed alive in me because I hadn't fully surrendered it to God, and this moment was a wake-up call. From that day forward, I knew I had to somehow close the door on fear completely, trusting God fully to carry me through. It was a pivotal step in reclaiming the freedom He had already given me.

In 2012, my mother, with whom I had a strained and tense relationship for many years due to the abuse I endured, was diagnosed with ovarian cancer. Despite our history, I didn't hesitate to step in alongside my youngest sister to take care of her. This four-year battle with cancer became an unexpected chapter of healing and redemption in our relationship. My mother had become a believer a few years before her illness. As she fought cancer, her faith deepened. She prayed daily, immersed herself in the Word, and attended church until her health no longer allowed it. Watching her lean into her faith while battling a disease that was slowly consuming her body was both heartbreaking and inspiring. I accompanied her to every chemo session, every hospital visit, and spent as much time as possible with her at home.

Although these days were marked by watching her endure unimaginable pain, they were also filled with moments of connection that restored our bond. I finally felt like I had my mother back—the mother I thought I had lost so many years ago. Yet, as I have shared throughout this journey, fear never left my side. When I left my ex-husband, fear didn't disappear; it simply found a new way to attack. As I watched my mother suffer, fear grew within me like a cancer of its own. I was terrified of losing her, of seeing her life slip away before my eyes. Her decision to stop treatment and accept hospice care was a turning point—not just for her, but for me as well.

During this time, I learned the power of acceptance. I accepted her decisions, I accepted that she would die, and

I trusted God's promise of peace and everlasting life for her. That acceptance didn't come easily or without an argument with God. I questioned Him: "Why would You give me my mother back, only to take her away? Why would You allow me to pray for her healing, only for her not to be healed?" But deep in my heart, I knew this wasn't punishment. I knew we all have a time to leave this earth, and I clung to the truth that to be absent from the body is to be present with the Lord (2 Corinthians 5:8).

In the end, I was grateful—grateful for the restoration of our mother-daughter relationship, grateful for the time we had, and even grateful that her suffering came to an end. In her final days, my mother spoke her last words to me: "I love you." After that, she didn't speak again. But I will never forget the moments just before she passed, as she looked upward, smiling and reaching out to something—or someone—I couldn't see with my natural eyes. Peace enveloped her in a way that I had never witnessed before. In that moment, I knew. God had sent His angels to comfort her and guide her transition from this life to eternal rest. Her passing was a profound moment of pain and peace intertwined, and it reminded me that even in loss, God's presence and promises remain.

As I look back on this time with my mother, I see it through a lens of understanding I didn't have before. Yes, she was afraid—after all, she was facing the unknown, staring death in the face. But here's the key: She did not allow fear to strip her of her faith. She leaned into God, holding on to His promises with unwavering trust. Fear only has the power you give it. My mother refused to grant it that power, even in her weakest moments. Another key realization came to me much later: God did answer my prayers for her healing. At the time, I struggled to understand why her physical body wasn't restored, but now I see the bigger picture. God did something far greater. He removed her suffering—not just from cancer but from the emotional and mental pain she had carried throughout her life. He healed the parts of her that no medical treatment could reach. Her healing was complete and eternal, freeing her from every chain that bound her on earth. This revelation has stayed with me as a reminder that God's answers to our prayers may not always come in the way we expect, but they always reflect His perfect plan and love. My mother's journey was a testament to the power of faith over fear and the ultimate healing that only God can provide.

When my mother passed away, fear once again found its way to the forefront of my life, whispering its lies and reminding me that I was still under its grip. Every ache and pain I felt became magnified, every discomfort twisted into the possibility of ovarian cancer. I found myself trapped in a cycle of anxiety and dread, replaying the memories of my mother's physical suffering like a haunting reel in my mind. I wept at every mammogram, trembling at every annual gynecological visit. The mere thought of following in her footsteps, enduring the tubes that sustained her body, the nausea that consumed her, the pain that marked her days—it paralyzed me. For five long years, I carried this paranoia like a weight on my shoulders. Every time a test result came back negative, I would cry tears of gratitude, but relief was fleeting. The cycle repeated itself with every new ache, every small symptom that bore the faintest resemblance to hers. This endless loop of fear and anxiety consumed me until one day, in the midst of my turmoil, I heard God's voice speak clearly and lovingly to my heart: "You are not your mother, and her life is not your life. Fear not and know that I am God."

In that moment, something shifted. It was as though God Himself had reached into the pit I was spiraling in and pulled me out. His words reminded me of a truth I had forgotten: I was not living my mother's story, and my future was not bound by the same pain she endured. Fear had no power except what I had given it, and God was calling me to let it go, to trust Him completely, and to walk in the freedom and peace He had for me. That day marked yet another step in my release from fear's chains. It didn't happen overnight, but the process began with those words from God—a reminder that He is greater than anything I could ever face and that His plans for me are rooted in His love, not fear.

Now, I have shared with you many of the traumatic events in my life—my battle with abuse, the loss of someone I loved deeply, and the lasting impact of her suffering on my own mental and emotional state. I've painted a picture of how fear seemed to hold an unrelenting power over me, dictating my decisions and keeping me bound. But here is what I want you to truly understand: Fear actually has no power at all. Let me be clear—this does not mean you will never feel afraid. Fear is an emotion, and it is part of the human experience. We all encounter moments that make us tremble or question what lies ahead. However, the question is not whether fear exists; it's whether fear has the authority to control your life. Does fear have the power to keep us in chains? The answer is both yes and no. Yes, fear can bind you—if you allow it. Fear thrives on the space you give it in your heart and mind. It gains strength when you feed it with doubt, insecurity, and inaction. But here's the truth: Fear is powerless when you deny it a seat at your table. It cannot control you if you refuse to let it feast on your mind, your body, and your spirit. What I've learned through my journey is that fear is a liar. It masquerades as powerful, but it's only as strong as the attention and authority you give it. Once you recognize that its power is an illusion, you can stand up, take back control, and claim the peace and freedom that God has already promised you.

The key is not to deny fear's existence but to deny it dominion over your life. When you replace fear with faith, you strip it of the ability to keep you in chains. That, my friend, is where true freedom begins. Spiritual warfare is an intense and deeply personal battle, often waged within the quiet corners of our minds and hearts. It manifests as doubt, fear, anxiety, or unexpected challenges that seem to arise from nowhere. These struggles are not merely coincidental—they are part of a larger, unseen conflict between good and evil forces, vying to influence our thoughts, emotions, and actions. This warfare requires vigilance and perseverance. It calls us to stand firm against the lies of the enemy, reject fear and discouragement, and cling to the truth that God has already secured the victory. By acknowledging the existence of this unseen battle, we equip ourselves to fight—not with our own strength but with the divine power that comes through faith, prayer, and unwavering reliance on God. Throughout my childhood and much of my adult life, I succumbed to fear. I allowed fear to stagnate my growth, to shape my decisions, and to reign over my life. But this wasn't merely a battle against an abuser or the paranoia of dying like my mother had—it was a spiritual battle. Fear wasn't just a feeling; it was a tool wielded by the enemy to keep me from walking in the purpose God had for me. When God creates us, He doesn't just create us to exist—He creates us with a purpose, a plan, a calling to fulfill His work. Fear is not part of His design for us.

The enemy, however, throws fear at us like a blazing fireball, attempting to engulf us in its consuming flames. In those moments, we have two choices: pick up the spiritual baseball bat of faith, truth, and the Word of God to knock that fireball out of the park, or stand still and allow ourselves to be hit, consumed by fear's destructive fire. Fear doesn't come from God, and it has no power unless we give it power. Spiritual warfare is about choosing to stand in the victory God has already won, trusting that His strength is enough to shield us from every attack and extinguish every fire the enemy throws our way. "Do not be afraid—I will save you. I have called you by name—you are mine. When you pass through deep waters, I will be with you; your troubles will not overwhelm you. When you pass through fire, you will not be burned; the hard trials that come will not hurt you. For I am the Lord your God, the holy God of Israel, who saves you." This powerful passage from Isaiah 43:1–3 was given to me by my spiritual mother many years ago.

At the time, I was deeply entrenched in the chaos of abuse, slowly dying inside from discouragement, hopelessness, and fear. When she shared these words, I understood their meaning on a surface level, and they served as a glimmer of hope—God's reminder of His promises. Yet, as comforting as they were, I didn't truly digest them. You see, we often approach the Bible as though it's merely a book, filled with stories and lessons. But the Bible is not just a book—it is a lifeline. It is a blueprint for living, a powerful weapon against the enemy, spiritual food for the soul, and living water to quench the deepest thirsts. The Word of God is life itself. On my journey, it took me a long time to realize that this passage wasn't just poetic encouragement—it was God speaking directly to me. He was telling me: "Hey, you do not have to be afraid. I did not give you a spirit of fear. I gave you power. I gave you truth. I gave you love. I gave you peace. Most importantly, I gave you ME. All you need to do is trust me, extend your hand, and I will pull you out of the raging sea of fear that is drowning you. I will save you."

This realization changed everything. The Word of God transformed from something I read to something I lived. Those promises weren't just words on a page—they became the foundation of my faith and the weapon I used to overcome fear. God's truth became my truth, and with it, I found the courage to trust Him completely, knowing that He was with me through every storm, every fire, and every trial.

Let's talk about trust. I knew I was instructed and encouraged to trust God. I understood what the Word said about trusting Him. But the lingering question in my heart was how? How do I trust when my entire life has conditioned me to brace for disappointment? How do I not fear that if I let go of the steering wheel, slide out of the driver's seat, and let God drive, I won't face more suffering, more problems, more hurt, or more disappointment? Here's the first thing I had to accept: God never promised we wouldn't face suffering. In fact, He made it clear in John 16:33 (NIV): "I have told you these things, so that in me you may have peace. In this world you will have trouble. But take heart! I have overcome the world."

When I think about Jesus—His life from the moment of His birth to His crucifixion—I'm struck by the depth of His suffering. Jesus suffered. He was rejected, criticized, judged, shunned, humiliated, tormented, betrayed, denied, tested, beaten, and crucified. The unspeakable pain, shame, and cruelty He endured are unimaginable. Yet, He endured it all. Even in His final hours, Jesus experienced profound emotional and spiritual anguish. In Luke 22:44, we see Him alone and sorrowful as He faced the overwhelming weight of what was to come. In His prayer, He cried out to God, asking, "Father, if You are willing, take this cup from me; yet not my will, but Yours be done" (Luke 22:42).

Jesus knew what lay ahead—not just the physical torment of the cross but the deep emotional and spiritual burden of carrying the sin of the world. In His humanity, He felt the weight of anxiety and the gravity of what was to come. But here's the extraordinary thing: He did not allow those feelings to consume Him. He did not let fear, anguish, or emotion rule over Him. Instead, Jesus pushed through the storm of His emotions and surrendered fully to the Father. He handed over the steering wheel of His life, declaring, "Your will be done." In this act of surrender, He modeled for us the ultimate trust in God's plan, even in the face of unimaginable suffering. Jesus teaches us that while we may feel fear or distress, we are not meant to be ruled by them. Instead, we are called to place our faith in the one who holds our future, trusting that His will is perfect and good.

How Did I Begin to Trust God?

As transparent as I can be with you right now, the answer is simple: I was tired. Tired of carrying the heavy weight of anxious thoughts and worry. Tired of being drained by the constant grip of fear that seemed to follow me every day. Most of all, I was tired of myself. I had been driving this vehicle of life for so long, refusing to ask for help, that I finally reached a point where I wanted to surrender my license. I was ready to let someone else take the wheel. That's when I began to tell God, "I need You to do it—all of it." It wasn't an overnight transformation, but it was the start of something real. I began to seek Him with intention and purpose. I started reading the Word—not just skimming it, but truly seeking to understand it. Each scripture became a lifeline, a piece of wisdom that started to fill the void within me. I also began listening to the teachings of those called to preach and teach His Word. And let me tell you, I didn't just hear their words; I let them take root in my spirit. I digested the messages they delivered, allowing them to shape my thoughts and actions. Most importantly, I prayed more and praised more. When I didn't know what to pray, I leaned into the Holy Spirit, asking for intercession on my behalf. I praised God even in my darkest moments. Have you ever heard the phrase, "Praise Him through the storm"?

It sounds so simple, but let me assure you—it's anything but easy. How do you sing praises, glorify His name, and lift your hands in worship when your heart feels weighed down by fear, discouragement, and exhaustion? For me, my fuel came from this simple truth: "Look at where I've been and look at where I am now." Every time I reflected on the storms I had already weathered, I found a spark of gratitude. That gratitude turned into worship. And through that worship, I began to trust. Trusting God didn't erase the storms, but it changed how I endured them. I was no longer navigating them on my own. I had surrendered my control and handed over the wheel to the One who already knew the destination. That surrender was the beginning of my freedom.

Reaching Out for Freedom

The burdens I carried were so heavy that I could no longer stand on my own. I was exhausted, depleted, and desperate for relief. All that I had learned about God—all the stories of His grace and mercy, the breakthroughs, the miracles, the lives transformed—I longed to experience it for myself. I wanted what others had testified to: freedom, peace, and the overwhelming love of a God who never abandons His children. I realized I couldn't keep living behind the wall I had built around my heart. That wall, built from years of fear, pain, and self-reliance, had become my prison. But in that moment of desperation, I made a decision. I was willing to knock out just one brick—just enough to reach out a single hand to God. And as I reached out, I hoped—no, I believed—that He would take hold of it. I believed He would pull me out of the bondage that fear had held over me for so many years. That small act of faith, that tentative reach, became the beginning of my freedom.

The Repetition of Freedom

By now, you've probably noticed that I've mentioned being free from fear multiple times throughout this book. No, it's not a mistake. It's intentional. My journey wasn't just about surviving the traumas and challenges I faced—it had a purpose. It wasn't only to give me a testimony but to demonstrate to you how, step by step, surrendering fully to God and allowing Him to take control brought me freedom. God's grace has been the thread running through every chapter of my life. His unending love for me, His unwavering faithfulness, and His immeasurable mercy delivered me from countless traumatic events. Time and time again, His grace reached me—not only rescuing me from the hands of the enemy but also from the consequences of my own foolish choices. This freedom wasn't instant, and it wasn't always easy. But each time I chose to trust Him, He proved Himself faithful, pulling me closer to the life He had designed for me all along—a life free from the chains of fear, hopelessness, and despair.

The Power of Choice

Let me say this to you: God can deliver us out of any bondage, but the truth is, we can also deliver ourselves into it. I've heard many people say, "Oh, the devil did it," or, "It's the devil's fault." But let me tell you, there are times when the devil is just sitting back, munching on movie theater popcorn, and watching us do it to ourselves! We give him far too much credit. You see, God has already equipped us with everything we need to live free. He gave us free will, the Word, a Savior, the promise of everlasting life, power, love, and a sound mind. The weapon of fear might creep up on us, but we have the authority to rebuke it. We have the power to deny it a seat at our table, to stop it from feasting on our thoughts, emotions, and peace. Or, we can choose to let it reside within us, rent-free. The choice is ours. God has already done His part—He's given us the tools and the promises. The question is, will we use them? Will we take authority over fear, or will we allow it to rule over us? Fear only has the power we give it. It's time to reclaim that power and remind fear that it has no place in the life of someone who walks with God.

The Power of Prayer

For a long time, I didn't know what it truly meant to pray. I would observe others praying and think, *Wow, their prayers are so powerful. The words are so strong, so bold. I don't know how to do that. Will God even receive my prayer if it's just simple wording?* During those 90 days when I found myself on my face, yelling and screaming out to God, I came to understand something that changed everything: There is no "right" way to pray. Prayer is not about perfect words or grand gestures—it's about talking to God. For me, prayer has become simply that—talking to my Father. I spend time with God even if it's just a moment of sharing a thought, a concern, or a question. I bring it to Him. God doesn't care about the eloquence of your words, the length of your prayer, or how "perfect" it sounds. He cares about the time you give Him, the sincerity of your heart, and your willingness to communicate with Him. Prayer isn't about impressing God with big words or long speeches. It's about opening your heart to Him, however simple it might be. Whether you're whispering a quick thought during a busy day or pouring out your soul in tears during a quiet moment, what matters is that you're bringing it to Him. That's all He asks.

The Fervent Effectual Prayer Availeth Much

Prayer is one of the most powerful tools we have as believers, yet too often, it's treated as a last resort—a cry to God only when we find ourselves in trouble or need. While God hears all our prayers, this kind of sporadic, need-based prayer does little to build a true relationship with Him. Imagine only reaching out to a friend or family member when you need something—never calling to check in, express gratitude, or simply spend time together. Over time, that relationship would feel shallow and one-sided. This is not the kind of prayer God desires from us. He calls us to fervent and effectual prayer. What does it mean to pray fervently and effectually? Fervent prayer is heartfelt, passionate, and persistent. It's not casual or routine but reflects a deep longing for God's presence and intervention. It comes from the depths of our hearts, driven by faith and trust in God's power. Effectual prayer is prayer rooted in God's will and promises. It aligns with His Word, demonstrating an understanding of who He is and His desire for our lives. It's not just asking for what we want but seeking His will to be done above all else. James 5:16 (KJV) tells us, "The effectual fervent prayer of a righteous man availeth much."

This means that when we pray with sincerity, faith, and alignment to God's will, our prayers have great power and produce significant results. Prayer is more than a transaction—it's a connection. Fervent and effectual prayer is an ongoing conversation with our Creator, a daily acknowledgment of our dependence on Him. It's where battles are won, hearts are transformed, and faith is strengthened. Don't wait for a crisis to approach God. Build your relationship with Him through constant, fervent, and effectual prayer. Call upon Him not just for what He can do but for who He is. The results will be life-changing—not just in your circumstances but in your spirit as well.

What Does It Mean to "Pray Without Ceasing"?

The Bible gives us this powerful instruction in 1 Thessalonians 5:17 (KJV): "Pray without ceasing." At first glance, this might seem like an impossible command. How can we pray continuously when life requires us to work, care for our families, and fulfill our daily responsibilities? To understand this verse, we need to look deeper into what Paul meant when he wrote these words.

Prayer as a Lifestyle!

Praying without ceasing doesn't mean we must be on our knees in formal prayer 24/7. Instead, it means cultivating a constant awareness of God's presence and maintaining an ongoing conversation with Him throughout our day. It's about living in a state of spiritual attentiveness, where prayer becomes as natural as breathing.

1. A Heart Posture of Dependence: To pray without ceasing is to live in continual reliance on God. It means acknowledging that we need Him in every aspect of our lives, big or small. By doing so, we develop a mindset of surrender, inviting God into our thoughts, decisions, and actions throughout the day.
2. Conversations, Not Just Requests: Prayer isn't limited to asking for things. It's a conversation with our Creator—a chance to praise, thank, and simply commune with Him. When we share our joys, burdens, and even our mundane thoughts with God,

we're practicing unceasing prayer.

3. Praying Through Our Actions: Prayer can also be reflected in how we live. When we serve others, work with integrity, or show love and kindness, these actions can be an expression of prayer, offering our lives as worship to God. As Colossians 3:23 (NIV) reminds us, "Whatever you do, work at it with all your heart, as working for the Lord."
4. A Habit of Gratitude: Praying without ceasing includes cultivating a grateful heart. When we see God's hand in our blessings and challenges, we can continually thank Him. Gratitude shifts our focus from worry to worship, helping us stay connected to God throughout the day.
5. Being Ready to Pray Anytime: Praying without ceasing means we're always ready to lift up a prayer—whether it's a quick word of thanks, a cry for help, or intercession for someone in need. It's about creating space in our hearts for God, no matter where we are or what we're doing.

Why Is It Important?

Praying without ceasing anchors us spiritually, reminding us of God's constant presence and our reliance on Him. It reassures us that we are never alone, helping to strengthen our faith, bring peace during life's challenges, and align our hearts with His purpose. This ongoing connection fosters trust in His guidance and provision.

Practical Ways to Pray Without Ceasing

Begin with gratitude: Start each morning by thanking God for His blessings and the gift of a new day.
Offer quick prayers throughout the day: Simple phrases like "Lord, help me" or "Thank You for being with me" help maintain a sense of connection.

Meditate on His Word: Reflect on Scripture, seeking God's insight into its meaning and application in your life.

Transform concerns into prayers: When worries arise, bring them to God in prayer, trusting Him to provide solutions and peace.

End your day in thanks: Close your day by reflecting on God's faithfulness and expressing appreciation for His guidance and care. Incorporating prayer into all aspects of daily life fosters a deeper relationship with God, offering strength and clarity to navigate life's challenges with His presence at the center. Continuous prayer isn't about the duration of each prayer but about maintaining a constant connection with God in your heart. It's an opportunity to make Him the focal point of your daily life, drawing on His strength, peace, and joy. When prayer becomes an integral part of your life, God transitions from being someone you turn to in times of crisis to someone you journey with in every moment.

I had to learn prayer. What I mean by this is, I had to come to understand that God was more than just a great power to cry out to in times of desperation. I had to learn that prayer wasn't just a tool for emergencies—it was the foundation for a relationship. I needed to speak to God about everything, not just when I wanted Him to fix it. The key word here is depend. But how could I depend on God when I didn't know how to depend on anyone else? Depending on others had always led to disappointment, rejection, and abandonment.

The idea of relying on someone—even God—felt foreign and impossible. Yet, I knew I needed to learn. I reached a point where I had no choice but to depend on Him. There was no one else to turn to. I had carried the weight of everything for so long that I was utterly exhausted. I was tired of being strong, tired of being in control, tired of managing everything on my own. I craved something bigger than me, stronger than me, more reliable than anything or anyone I had ever known. I needed God. I desired Him to be the protector and provider over my life. So, I prayed. Not every day—sometimes not even every week. But I prayed because I wanted to trust Him. I wanted to lean on Him. I wanted God. My prayer life grew over time, not out of obligation but out of necessity. I began to speak to Him, not just with scripted words, but with raw honesty. I poured out my fears, my hopes, and my doubts. I shared my struggles and even my failures. Prayer became less about asking God for things and more about knowing Him. It became my way of leaning on Him, of saying, "I can't do this alone anymore." Through prayer, I started to see glimpses of what it meant to depend on God—not as a last resort, but as my first and only source of strength. It wasn't easy, but each time I surrendered a little more of my control, I found myself leaning into Him just a little more. And that made all the difference.

When I was in high school, a trend began circulating among my classmates—one that would change my perspective on the unseen world forever. One day, a girl brought a Ouija board to school. I watched as a group of my peers gathered in the locker room, sitting cross-legged on the floor, moving a small triangular planchette across the board. They giggled and whispered as it seemed to spell out answers to their questions. At first, I dismissed it as a silly game. I thought, *Surely, they're moving it themselves, spelling out the answers they want to hear.* But something about the board captivated me. It wasn't just the novelty; it was the promise of answers—something I deeply craved. So, I went out and bought one for myself. I brought it home and sat alone in my bedroom, eager to test its validity. I asked questions, resting my fingers lightly on the planchette. Nothing happened at first. Part of me was relieved, but another part—fueled by curiosity—urged me to keep trying. Then, it happened. The planchette began to move. Slowly at first, then with startling speed. It spelled out a name: Helen. Helen told me she was a young girl who had died in a fire in the 1800s. She spoke gently, even about God. She became my companion, giving me what seemed to be positive messages about my life and my future. I was captivated—so much so that I spent hours with the board every day after school, well into the early hours of the morning. My mother noticed my obsession and became concerned. She warned me to stop, but I didn't listen.

To me, Helen wasn't just a spirit; she was a friend who filled the void of loneliness I felt. But what seemed friendly at first quickly turned sinister. One day, the messages changed. The kind words disappeared, replaced with threats. Helen claimed she would kill me. Soon, the name Helen vanished, replaced by others—dark, menacing names. These spirits told me I would die. Terror consumed me. I took the board and broke it in half, throwing it away in the trash. The next morning, I watched the garbage truck haul it away, relieved to be free of its grasp—or so I thought. What I didn't realize at the time was that the Ouija board was more than a game. It was a gateway to the spirit world—a doorway to forces that were not of God. The Bible warns us clearly: "Do not turn to mediums or necromancers; do not seek them out, and so make yourselves unclean by them: I am the Lord your God" (Leviticus 19:31). "And no wonder, for even Satan disguises himself as an angel of light" (2 Corinthians 11:14). Deuteronomy 18:10-12 warns, "Let no one be found among you ... who practices divination or sorcery, interprets omens, engages in witchcraft, or casts spells, or who is a medium who consults the dead. Anyone who does these things is detestable to the Lord."

Even though I had thrown the board away, its grip on me wasn't broken. I couldn't stop thinking about it. I longed for the connection it gave me, despite the fear it brought. I made a new board out of cardboard, convincing myself it wouldn't work. But it did. The dark pull was back, stronger than ever. Deep inside, I knew I needed to break free. Here's why I'm sharing this story with you: Even in my fear, I had a small, flickering faith—a mustard seed of belief in the power of God. I didn't fully understand prayer, but I knew enough to cry out for help. I prayed with urgency, rebuking the power of the board and declaring myself a child of God. I demanded the spirits to leave and for the door I had opened to be closed. And just like that, it stopped. The longing was gone. The pull vanished.

I threw the makeshift board away and never looked back. In that moment, I trusted the power of prayer. It wasn't eloquent. It wasn't perfect. But it was earnest, and it was filled with faith—just enough faith for God to intervene and deliver me. As I think about it, this experience taught me that while the enemy is real and his tactics are deceptive, the power of God is greater. Prayer isn't just a ritual; it's a weapon. And when we use it, we invite God's authority to close every door the enemy tries to pry open in our lives. The power of prayer is real, and it is stronger than anything that comes against us.

What Did Prayer Do for Me?

Prayer transformed my focus—it shifted my perspective from being consumed by my circumstances to trusting in what I needed God to do to change those circumstances. It was a deliberate act of reliance on His power and faithfulness rather than my own limited strength. Through prayer, I drew closer to God. I often heard others, including my spiritual mother, say that God had spoken to them. I would wonder, *How? How does God speak? Is that even possible?* But as I began building my relationship with God, I realized that He speaks in many ways—through people, through scriptures, and through a quiet voice in my spirit.

This voice is indescribable, but unmistakably God. Prayer brought me into the very presence of God. In those moments, I felt His ears tuned into my heart's cries, and His Holy Spirit surrounded and filled me, both externally and internally. It became my direct communication with God—not only for my own needs but to intercede on behalf of the ones I love. Lastly, prayer became my weapon against fear. It calmed my restless spirit, quieted my anxious thoughts, and reminded me of the power I had access to through my relationship with God. It wasn't just an act of speaking to God; it was an act of surrender and trust that brought peace to my soul.

A Powerful Testament to the Power of Prayer

Let me share a moment that forever solidified my belief in the power of prayer. When my son, Shawn, was just two years old, he accidentally swallowed paint thinner. I was upstairs when the incident occurred. Shawn had found a soda bottle on the edge of a shelf in a family member's bedroom—a bottle no one realized contained paint thinner, left there by her youngest child. As soon as he drank it, his throat immediately closed, and his lungs collapsed. I will never forget the panic that consumed me as I raced downstairs to the chaos of screams and confusion. My family frantically explained that Shawn had swallowed something dangerous. His small, lifeless body was blue, and I knew time was running out. My CPR training kicked in as I tried everything I could, but nothing worked.

Helpless and terrified, I screamed for someone—anyone—to save my baby. His father and uncle grabbed him from my arms and ran out the door, racing to the hospital. Fear paralyzed me. I was frozen, unable to process what was happening. But my spiritual mother? She wasted no time waging her battle. Her weapon? Prayer. She cried out to God, pleading for His intervention. She rebuked the devil and declared that my son was a child of God who would not be taken. Her faith was unwavering, her prayers fervent and commanding. By the time I arrived at the hospital, a doctor was shouting, demanding to know what substance Shawn had ingested. "Smell his shirt! What is this?" he asked. The chemical smell was overwhelming, and I frantically called home, yelling at my family in desperation. "What was left where he could reach it? Did someone leave nail polish remover?" No one knew. Later, we discovered it was paint thinner. But what I want you to focus on is not the chaos—it's the outcome. The outcome was nothing short of miraculous, and I know it was because of God and the power of prayer. Shawn had stopped breathing long enough to risk brain damage. His lungs were collapsed, his throat singed. The prognosis was grim.

Yet, within a two-week stay at the hospital, doctors were amazed. They described his recovery as if nothing had ever happened. Every test, every scan showed healing that defied medical explanation. During those two weeks, my spiritual mother never ceased praying. She knelt daily, covering Shawn in anointing oil during her hospital visits and declaring his healing. I remember one particular moment when the nurse explained that Shawn had refused to eat despite her countless attempts. My mother smiled and replied, "God is going to turn that around." She prayed over him, and when the nurse returned, Shawn was peacefully drinking a warm bottle of milk in her arms. His medicine was prayer. His healing was God's grace. That moment reminded me that when we are powerless, God's power is limitless. Prayer isn't just words; it's the bridge to divine intervention. It saved my son's life.

A New Chapter in Georgia

In 2021, my husband and I made a monumental decision to uproot our lives and move to Georgia. The purpose was clear: to help a sick family member get back on their feet. It was a decision made out of love, one we believed was worth sacrificing everything we had worked for. However, what began as an act of selflessness quickly turned into a season of heartache and storms we hadn't anticipated. Amid these challenges, my son, Matthew, who has an incredible knowledge of churches and pastors across the country, discovered that a pastor he had briefly met in Delaware had started a church in Georgia. After attending a few services, Matthew urged me to join him. I hesitated.

My past experiences with churches had left me feeling disconnected and unsure—many didn't feel like places where God truly dwelled. Reluctantly, I agreed to go. From the moment I stepped into this small, welcoming church,

I was greeted with warmth and love by the congregation, including the Apostle. The outpouring of genuine kindness overwhelmed me, bringing me to tears. It was here, in this humble little sanctuary, that God began to speak to me more clearly than ever before. Through the Apostle and other leaders in the church, God revealed a truth about me that I had yet to fully grasp: I am called to be an intercessor, someone with the power of prayer to stand in the gap for others.

Let me be honest—this revelation didn't bring instant joy or excitement. Instead, it brought fear. Yes, fear. There it was again, rearing its head just when I was beginning to take steps forward. I thought to myself, *Really, God? Me? Are You sure?* Here I was, still working on fully believing that my prayers weren't just for others but for myself, too. I was just starting to acknowledge that God truly hears me, that He genuinely loves me. And now I'm being told I have a calling so significant, so weighty? Fear gripped me—not of the calling itself but of inadequacy. I wondered, *What if I'm not enough? What if I don't live up to this calling? What if I fail?*

But even in that fear, God was patient. He was teaching me that He didn't call me because I was perfect or had it all together. He called me because I was willing, even in my hesitation. This was the beginning of a new journey—one where I would learn to not only trust God with my prayers but to trust Him with the very calling He placed on my life. A calling that required me to let go of fear and embrace His purpose, knowing He equips those He calls. I would often find myself reflecting on the story of Moses, especially when doubt and fear crept into my thoughts. When God called Moses to be His messenger, to lead His people out of bondage, Moses hesitated.

He didn't feel equipped for such an enormous task. He doubted his abilities and questioned his worthiness for the role. In Exodus 4:10 (NLT), Moses said to the Lord, "O Lord, I'm not very good with words. I never have been, and I'm not now, even though you have spoken to me. I get tongue-tied, and my words get tangled."

Can you imagine? God Himself was speaking directly to Moses, calling him to fulfill an extraordinary purpose, and yet Moses focused on his limitations rather than God's power. He felt inadequate, unworthy, and incapable of delivering the message. This resonates deeply with me because I, too, felt unprepared when I began to realize the calling God had placed on my life. Like Moses, I looked at my shortcomings. I thought about the times I had failed, the doubts I carried, and the fear that whispered, "You're not good enough." But just as God assured Moses that He would be with him, providing the words and strength needed, I began to understand that God wasn't asking me to rely on my own abilities. He was asking me to trust Him. Exodus 4:12 (NLT) says, "Now go! I will be with you as you speak, and I will instruct you in what to say."

God doesn't call the qualified; He qualifies the called. Moses' story is a reminder that our limitations are irrelevant when God's power is at work within us. It's not about what we bring to the table but about our willingness to say yes to

God's call, knowing He will provide everything we need to accomplish His purpose. Moses' journey encouraged me to stop focusing on my inadequacies and start trusting in God's sufficiency. If He could use Moses—a man who doubted himself so deeply—to lead an entire nation, surely He could use me, even with all my imperfections. I would listen to leaders, the Apostle, and other members of the congregation pray with such power and confidence, their words flowing effortlessly as though they had been born for this. Meanwhile, I would shrink back, convinced I could never sound like them. Just the thought of speaking in front of the congregation left me nervous and tongue-tied. I couldn't help but relate to Moses, who told God, "I'm not very good with words. I never have been, and I'm not now" (Exodus 4:10, NLT).

How could God possibly think I could do this? What was my Apostle thinking, believing I was capable of standing in such a role? Could they not see the person I was—the fear, the self-doubt, the uncertainty? But that's just it—God sees me. He sees what I cannot yet see in myself. My Apostle, guided by the Spirit, saw beyond my insecurities and into the potential God had placed within me. The truth was, it wasn't about my own abilities but about what God could do through me. I was the only one standing in the way of seeing myself through the lens of God's purpose. Here's one thing I know about myself: I will not knowingly defy God. If God says, "Do it," then I'm going to do it—whether I feel confident or not. Even if I think I'm doing a terrible job, obedience is non-negotiable for me.

So, whenever I'm called to pray, I go. Why? Because I trust God. I may still be working on fully believing in myself, but my faith in God is unwavering. Here's the thing—you can't ask God to deliver you from fear while continuing to let fear dictate your life. Fear is a weapon, and if you allow it, it will hinder you. It will keep you stagnant, stop your growth, and discourage the success that's meant for you. Worse yet, fear can block you from walking in the promises of God. But I don't want fear to hold me back. I want everything God has promised me. I want to become everything God says I'm meant to be. And most of all, I want God—fully, completely. I want less of me and more of Him. Trusting Him, even when I feel uncertain, is how I keep moving forward. Obedience is my answer to fear, and faith is the weapon I use to conquer it. Hebrews 10:36 reminds us: "You need to persevere so that when you have done the will of God, you will receive what He has promised." Perseverance through faith and trust in God's guidance ensures that His promises will come to pass in our lives. Fear may try to stop us, but with obedience and unwavering faith, we move forward—closer to the fulfillment of God's will.

CHAPTER 4

The Power of Unwavering Faith

A Story of Loss and Trust

In 2023, my family faced a tragedy so profound it shook the very foundation of our lives. A fire broke out in the home my spiritual mother had cherished for 54 years—a home where she raised her children, took in the homeless (including myself at one point), and poured her heart and soul into building a legacy of love and care. This was a home filled with memories, laughter, and the fruits of her hard work. And in the quiet hours of the morning, it was engulfed in flames. While my mother miraculously made it out of the fire unharmed, my sister was trapped inside. When the firefighters finally reached her, she was unresponsive. She was rushed to the hospital and placed on life support. For two agonizing weeks, we surrounded her in prayer, hoping for a miracle—that she would breathe on her own, wake up, and return to us. But that miracle didn't come.

My sister, at 67 years old, left us to be with the Lord. The loss was unbearable, especially for my mother. My sister had been her best friend, her caregiver, and a beacon of love and kindness. She spent her life helping others—feeding the hungry, lending a hand to anyone in need, caring for children, and even ensuring elderly women safely boarded the bus. She was truly an angel on earth, and her absence left a void none of us could fill. But amidst the ashes of this tragedy, the true power of faith emerged. My mother, at 94 years old, watched as everything she held dear was taken from her—the home she built, the memories she cherished, and her beloved daughter. Yet, she did not lose her faith. She did not turn away from God.

Instead, she turned toward Him with fervent prayers, asking for strength, understanding, and peace. I remember her sharing with me a moment of profound revelation. She asked God, "Why did You take her and not me?" And God, in His infinite wisdom, replied, "She is My daughter. I loaned her to you, but it was time for her to return to Me." My mother accepted this answer, knowing that God was not punishing her but fulfilling His divine plan. She leaned on His promises, trusting that He would restore what was lost. God assured her that she would never have to worry about a bill again when her restoration came. And through her grief—the anger, the sadness, the denial—she never wavered in her trust in the Lord. She prayed fervently, not just for herself but for her family, demonstrating an unshakable reliance on God even in her darkest hour. Her faith in the midst of such overwhelming loss taught me a lesson I will carry forever. She showed me that no matter how devastating the storm, trusting God can overcome every fear, heal every trauma, and carry you through to the other side.

My mother's unwavering faith, her ability to stand firm in

God's promises, and her reliance on prayer are a testament to the power of believing in Him wholeheartedly. It is a legacy of faith I will never forget. I can only imagine the magnitude of fear my mother must have felt as flames and smoke engulfed her room, the crackling sound of the roof beam collapsing, missing her frail body by mere inches. The chaos, the heat, the overwhelming sense of danger—all of it must have been terrifying beyond words. Yet, in that moment of impending disaster, she fought the only way she knew how.

My nephew, with courage and urgency, managed to reach her and pull her out to safety. But even before his arrival, her first response was to cry out the name that held the power to save: "Jesus!" In her fear, she didn't falter. She knew where her strength came from. "Jesus, save me!" she cried, and He did. That name—so powerful, so full of grace—became her shield in a moment when all seemed lost. Even in the face of such overwhelming terror, her faith became her weapon, and it carried her to safety. This moment reminds me that faith isn't just about trusting in the good times; it's about calling on Him in the darkest, scariest moments and knowing that He will answer. My mother's cry wasn't just a plea—it was an act of faith, and it was her faith that saved her.

This story is a testament to the boundless faithfulness of God and the lessons He gently teaches us through our trials. I often reflect on how I would cry out to God without hesitation for those I loved and wanted to protect, yet I struggled so deeply to believe He would show up for me, just for me. It was as if I had somehow convinced myself that my cries for others were worth hearing, but mine alone were not. When my twin sons were 11 years old, we faced a dire situation that forever changed my understanding of God's providence and my own need to surrender. I had recently started a new job working with the developmentally disabled population—a position I was excited about and grateful for. But only a few weeks in, my ex-husband took our car, leaving me stranded without money or a way to get to work. He disappeared for two weeks, and during that time, I missed too many shifts. The result? I was terminated from my job. One day, as my sons played outside, one of them came upstairs and innocently asked, "Mom, I'm hungry. What's for lunch?"

The question pierced my heart. I managed to hold back the overwhelming wave of emotions threatening to consume me. Calmly, I replied, "I'll prepare lunch and call you in when it's ready." What my son didn't know was that the refrigerator held nothing but a stick of butter, and the cabinets were nearly empty, save for a single box of macaroni and cheese. I had nothing else to offer my children. Shame and pride kept me from asking for help. My landlord, a kind woman, lived just downstairs. My best friend was only a block away. My biological mother and sister were an hour's drive from me. But no one knew how desperate our situation was because I was determined to fix everything on my own. That determination, however, had left me at a breaking point. I was desperate. With no car, no job, no money, and no options, I fell to my knees and cried out to God: "Please help me feed my children."

And God responded. Out of the blue, my best friend's sister—someone I rarely saw—called me. She explained that she had an overabundance of food and felt led to share it. She said, "I thought of you and your boys right away. Would it be okay if I dropped off some food at your house?"

Fighting back tears, I agreed, thanking her as calmly as I could. When she arrived, she brought multiple bags of groceries—enough to feed us for a week. I held my composure while she was there, not sharing my circumstances, but the moment she left, I broke down. I cried tears of gratitude, and I thanked God for His provision. I also realized something profound: God had heard me, but He was also teaching me to humble myself and ask for support. That same day, I went downstairs to my landlord and poured out the truth of my situation. I expected judgment or rejection, but instead, she handed me the keys to her car and told me to go to social services for emergency assistance.

Knowing I hadn't paid the month's rent, her generosity shocked me. But she didn't stop there—she handed me her credit card and told me to buy groceries. She even offered to help with transportation until I could resolve the situation. This was God's faithfulness in action. Through the kindness of others, He provided for my immediate needs and gently reminded me that humility and trust in Him open doors. That day, I learned that while God is always faithful, sometimes He asks us to step out in faith and lean on the community He places around us. We are not meant to carry our burdens alone. His love comes through His people, and His provision is constant—even when we least expect it. Fear had a firm grip on me. It lingered, deep inside, whispering doubts and keeping me silent. Fear of being judged or criticized for the situation I found myself in. Fear of what my ex-husband might do if he found out I had told anyone what was happening in our home. Fear of rejection from those I might ask for help, afraid they would turn me away or pity me in a way that felt unbearable. Fear kept me from uttering the one word that could have lightened my burden: HELP. Instead of reaching out, I chose to carry the weight alone, convincing myself that it was safer to endure silently than to risk vulnerability.

Fear, like a stubborn shadow, followed me into every decision, dictating my actions and keeping me from fully embracing the support God was offering through those around me. Looking back, I can see how fear robbed me of peace and added unnecessary pain to an already difficult season. But even then, God was patient. He waited for me to let go of fear's hold, and when I finally did, His love and provision were already there, waiting to catch me.

CHAPTER 5

FEAR

THE UNYIELDING GRIP

When I think about how fear has controlled most of my life, I see it as an unrelenting force, whispering doubt into every corner of my existence. Fear of man, fear of pain, fear of losing my mother, fear of losing my siblings, fear that the very male figures meant to protect me might instead end my life. Fear of being homeless, fear of not having enough food, fear of not succeeding, fear of not having enough money. Fear of not finding love without rejection or abandonment, fear of not measuring up, fear of not pleasing God. Fear of not being pretty enough, interesting enough, skinny enough. Fear that I won't work hard enough to provide, fear of saying the wrong thing, fear of not following through.

Fear of not being good enough to step into the purpose God has called me to. Fear of dying, fear of sickness, fear of others in my life dying, fear of loss in all its forms. It feels like fear upon fear, endlessly piling on, suffocating me under its weight. But as I truly reflect on all of this, I realize my biggest fear—the one that stands above all others—is this: fear of letting go of the steering wheel and trusting

God fully. *Will He provide? Will He protect? Will He shelter me? Will He hear me? Will He approve of me? Will He see me? Will He deliver me? Will He honor my prayers?* The question that lingers, echoing in my soul, is simply, *Will He?*

Growing up and even during my first marriage, the damaging words thrown at me dug deep wounds into my self-esteem and self-worth. "You're ugly," "You're stupid," "No one will ever want you," "You're never going to be anything," "You're fat," "You're this," "You're that"—everything was said to break me down. Although I tried to convince myself that those words meant nothing, considering the people they came from, deep down inside, they planted seeds of doubt. A voice inside whispered, *Maybe they're right. Maybe I'll never be worthy of anything more than what I have right now.*

Those words didn't just hurt in the moment; they lingered. They grew into fears that loomed over me, whispering lies that maybe I wasn't enough, that maybe I would never be enough. Those words didn't just damage my self-worth; they became fuel for fear to thrive. Fear used those words to keep me bound, to make me believe that stepping out, dreaming for more, or even hoping for better was futile. Fear used those wounds to keep me chained to the lie that I was unworthy, undeserving, and incapable of more. As I sit here writing, I ask God, "How do I explain to someone who suffered as a child that You were there? How do I help them understand that it wasn't You who punished them, abandoned them, or rejected them during such traumatic events?" These are heavy questions, and for me, the answer lies in looking back on my own life. When I reflect on every trial, tribulation, and storm I've faced—call me crazy—but I thank God. Why? Not because I rejoice in the fact that I was raped, beaten, molested, cheated on, homeless, stolen from, lied to, abandoned, rejected, or psychologically tormented. Of course not. Those experiences were devastating, and I wouldn't wish them on anyone. But my life, my journey, my trials, and my trauma have given me something invaluable: a testimony.

A testimony is a personal account of one's story and of God's grace, mercy, and power to transform or deliver. My testimony is not worthless. It's not useless. It's not in vain. It is evidence—evidence that God does love you, does hear you, does deliver, and will transform your life, your inner being, your mind, your body, and everything surrounding your existence if you trust Him. The very experiences that threatened to break me are now the foundation of my testimony. They allow me to speak to others with empathy, to share the power of God's intervention, and to give hope to those who feel abandoned or rejected. I don't thank God for the pain itself—or maybe I'm even grateful for it because it molded me into who I am—I thank Him for the ways He has used it to reveal His presence and power in my life.

My scars are the proof that I survived, and my testimony is the evidence that He was with me through it all. The sad reality is this: We live in a world that birthed sin. As people, we have been given the gift of free will—a precious gift from God that allows us to make choices, for better or worse. It's a gift intended to reflect His love and trust in us, but one that has also opened the door for pain and suffering.

God never promised us a life without hardship. In fact, He offered humanity a life free of suffering—a perfect existence in the Garden of Eden. But we chose, by our own desire, to disobey Him.

That single act of disobedience birthed a world where right and wrong coexist, a world where sin gave Satan the opportunity to influence, manipulate, and discourage us in both mind and body. When children suffer, it is not by the hand of God but by the hand of man, influenced by the brokenness of sin. Sin unleashed the potential for evil in the world, and humanity, in its free will, has often chosen paths that lead to harm and destruction. This is not a reflection of God's will but of the misuse of the freedom He has granted us. Now, you might ask, "Why doesn't God stop it? Doesn't He have the power to end all suffering?" Of course, He does. But if God were to operate in that way, overriding every decision and controlling every action, would we truly have free will? Would we be the beings He created us to be—capable of love, growth, and transformation—or would we be robots? No choices, no decisions, no dreams, no goals, no passions. Just human robots, programmed and controlled by God.

God's love for us is evident in the freedom He allows, even knowing the risks it entails. He does not force Himself upon us but instead invites us to choose Him, to align our free will with His perfect will. It's a heartbreaking reality that suffering exists, but it also serves as a reminder of the profound gift of choice and the eternal hope we have in God's plan for restoration and redemption. He doesn't leave us to navigate this broken world alone—He walks with us, offering His strength, His comfort, and His promise of a world made new. I have been a mental health professional in behavioral health for over 20 years. In those years, I gained extensive knowledge about how trauma affects us psychologically. Naturally, when faced with a frightening or life-threatening situation, our brains respond with anxiety and fear, triggering the fight, flight, or freeze response.

This is the brain's way of signaling danger and preparing the body to react. However, as someone who has survived many traumas in my own life, I can tell you that even after the immediate danger is gone, the remnants of those traumas often linger. I went through therapy, had countless conversations with men and women of God, and did the work to heal. Yet, I still carried those remnants with me. I've seen the same in many clients throughout my professional career—clients who have sought therapy, taken medication, and done everything within their power to feel "normal," only to find the struggle remains. Through these observations, I've noticed a common denominator: Many of these individuals either don't believe there's truly a God, don't trust Him, or don't know how to trust Him. Let's pause for a moment to dive deeper into what trust really means. Trust is a firm belief in the reliability, truth, ability, or strength of someone or something. The funny thing about trust is that we so often place it in things and people without being able to see or touch it tangibly. I recently had a conversation with my husband, Michael, that illustrated this beautifully. I gave him a scenario: "Michael, if we were being chased by a group of people seeking to take our lives, and we reached the edge of a cliff with a body of water far below, you'd likely say, 'Baby, we have to jump into the water because there's no other way out.' My response would be, 'But I can't swim.' You'd then tell me, 'Trust me. I'll hold on to you, and I'll swim us to safety.'"

I explained to him that although I'd be terrified, I would trust him. I would take the leap, not because I had any guarantee of the outcome, but because I know his character, his love for me, and his promise to protect me. I would put aside my fear, trust his words, and take the risk. This scenario might sound dramatic, but it perfectly encapsulates what it means to put trust into action. In this situation, my trust in my husband would override my fear because I believe in his intention and ability to save me. Now, think about this in terms of our relationship with God. Trusting God works in a similar way—it's about believing in His character, His promises, and His unfailing love, even when the outcomes aren't immediately clear. It's about letting go of our fear and taking the leap, knowing that God's hands are the safest place we could ever be. I think about the day I left my ex-husband. I was terrified. As I hurried my sons to get dressed and gather their necessities, I remember pacing outside the home, my heart racing as I scanned the road, watching for any sign of him driving up.

Rationally, I knew he wouldn't be coming home at that time—he was likely sleeping off his drunkenness in the bed of his mistress. But fear doesn't always listen to reason. It kept me on edge, whispering doubts and heightening my anxiety. Even so, I fought the voice of fear. I pushed through it, focusing on trusting that God would keep us safe as we left. In that moment, I trusted God. I trusted His promises, His character, and His love. But let me tell you, this wasn't easy. I fought every urge to stop moving forward. I fought to ignore the relentless voice in my head telling me, *This is the wrong decision. He will find you.* And then, there was another layer of trust that I had to confront: trusting the friend who offered us refuge.

That wasn't easy for me, either. After all, we weren't particularly close. We barely spent time together over the years, and I had only just confided in her about my situation. I had to trust that she truly meant it when she said she would help. I had to trust that she wouldn't throw us out after a day or two, and that she would stand by me as I navigated the daunting tasks ahead—securing a restraining order, finding a new place to live, and sorting out finances. If you think that trusting her came naturally, let me assure you it did not. My life up until that point had been a series of traumas and disappointments, teaching me over and over again that people don't always follow through on their promises. But this time, I pushed through my doubts and accepted her help, even with all my reservations. When I look back now, I see it clearly: I wasn't just trusting her—I was trusting God. I was trusting Him to not only protect me and my sons but also to provide for us. And He did. He provided through her, someone I wouldn't have expected. Someone I didn't have a close bond with. Someone who had already been used by God a few years earlier to bring me bags of food when I had no way to feed my children.

God showed me, once again, that He can use anyone, even the least expected person, to fulfill His promise to care for us. That day, despite my fear and doubts, I stepped out in faith—and God met me there. He provided the protection, the refuge, and the help I needed to begin rebuilding my life. The parable in Luke 4:8–15 resonates deeply with me, particularly when I reflect on my journey of learning to trust God. Each stage of my life has mirrored the different outcomes of the seed in this story. There was a time when I was like the seed that fell by the roadside. I would go to church, hear the Word, and even feel moved in the moment. But as soon as I left, the Word would be snatched away by my own distractions, poor choices, or circumstances. I didn't allow it a chance to take root in my heart. Later, I resembled the seed that fell on rocky soil. I heard the Word and received it with joy. I prayed and sought God in moments of clarity. But when challenges arose—when fear crept in, when life didn't go as I had hoped—I quickly abandoned my faith. I let the weight of my troubles overpower the truth of God's promises.

There were also times when I was like the seed among thorny weeds. I prayed, attended church, and even sought God's guidance, but my worries, anxieties, and doubts choked the life out of the Word that was planted. I allowed fear to wrap around me so tightly that it left no room for growth. Instead of trusting God, I clung to my circumstances, letting them dictate my actions and my faith. Now, as I look at my journey, I am grateful for transformation. Today, I strive to be like the seed that fell on good soil. I no longer just hear the Word—I let it nourish me. I trust in the Living

Water and allow God's teachings to penetrate deeply into my life. This trust is not always easy, but it has become the foundation of my growth. The soil of my heart has been tilled through trials, watered by God's grace, and warmed by His love. I seek to produce good fruit—not just for my benefit but to glorify Him and be a blessing to others.

My journey has shown me that when we truly trust in God, we can grow beyond the limits of our circumstances. The Word becomes our nourishment, our guide, and our strength, allowing us to live a life that bears fruit in every season. Let me caution you: It is so easy to slip back into being the seed that doesn't grow or the seed that produces no fruit. And let me tell you, the devil counts on it! Having faith and continuously trusting God is a daily journey. Why? Because we never know what tomorrow might bring. Life is unpredictable, and challenges will come. But as we build on our relationship with the Father, we grow in our knowledge of who He is, what He has already done, and what we believe He will do. God understands that we are only human. Why does He understand? Because He gave us His Son, Jesus, to experience life as a human and to feel the same emotions and challenges we face. God loved us so much that He presented Himself in His Son to fully grasp the human experience. When you think of Jesus, do you find yourself passively saying, "Well, He was the Son of God, He was our Savior, and He had the power of God, so of course, He doesn't really understand how hard it is to trust"? If so, let me stop you right there. That kind of thinking is a lie!

If you've read your Bible, studied the Word, or even just heard about the life of Christ, you'll know that this passive perspective couldn't be further from the truth. Jesus suffered—not just on the cross and not just on the road to Calvary, but throughout His life. His journey was filled with emotional and physical pain brought on by the actions and rejection of others. He was rejected, hungry, lonely, sad, anxious, angry, and even taunted. He experienced so many of the struggles we face today. So, yes, He absolutely understands our hardships and our struggles to trust. Think about the 40-day fast. Here was Jesus, in the wilderness, physically exhausted and deprived of nourishment. And during this time of extreme vulnerability, the devil taunted Him, whispering lies, trying to sow seeds of doubt. Can you imagine that? Have you ever been truly hungry—so hungry that it wasn't just physical but also mental and emotional exhaustion? Jesus experienced that, too. But despite the taunts and temptations, Jesus stood firm. He trusted God. He held fast to God's Word, knowing it was his shield and armor. He is our ultimate example of what it means to trust, even when circumstances and emotions scream otherwise.

So, let me encourage you: Trust isn't passive, and it isn't always easy. It's an active choice we make every single day. And when we feel weak or uncertain, we can look to Jesus, who fully understands our struggles and offers us the strength to persevere. I've heard people ask, "How do you trust in a God you don't hear or see?" Let's break that down for a moment. We trust in air—yes, I know this example is often used, but it's true.

Every time we inhale, we trust that our body will receive the oxygen it needs to keep us alive. We don't see it, but we trust it. Let's look at other examples: When you work 40 hours a week and have your paycheck set up for direct deposit, you trust that when you check your bank account, the money will be there. You're not the one manually putting the money into the account. Some person or technology is handling that transaction. Yet, you trust that it'll be there. When you get into your car and turn the key, you trust that the engine will start. Sure, things can go wrong—a dead battery, a mechanical issue—but even when those obstacles arise, you trust that the mechanic will fix it. When your paycheck doesn't show up in your account, you trust that the payroll department will resolve the issue once you notify them.

Here's the thing: God never said we wouldn't face obstacles. He never promised that life would be without suffering or challenges. What He did promise is that we could trust Him to see us through those challenges. Even when we don't see the solution, He already has it. Now, let's flip this scenario: The mechanic tells you, "Bring me the car, and I'll fix it." The payroll department assures you, "Notify us, and we'll correct the issue."

You trust them, right? But here's the real question: Why do we trust the mechanic or the payroll department but not God? The mechanic, as skilled as they may be, didn't create the car. The payroll department, efficient as they may be, didn't create your job or the resources that sustain you. Yet we place so much trust in these human systems. And then there's God—the Creator of all things. The Provider of all things. The Healer of all things. The One who has a perfect track record of faithfulness. Yet, when it comes to trusting Him, we hesitate. Make it make sense!

How can we trust "Barney the mechanic" or ADP Payroll but struggle to trust the One who holds the entire universe in His hands? Trusting God isn't about what we can see or hear; it's about knowing who He is and believing in His promises, even when we don't fully understand the process. God has given you the power to overcome fear. He has equipped you to fight the lies of the enemy. He has made you more than a conqueror, and He has provided you with the full armor to battle and win! "Finally, be strong in the Lord and in his mighty power. Put on the full armor of God so that you can take your stand against the devil's schemes. For our struggle is not against flesh and blood, but against the rulers, against the authorities, against the powers of this dark world and against the spiritual forces of evil in the heavenly realms."

Therefore, put on the full armor of God, so that when the day of evil comes, you may be able to stand your ground, and after you have done everything, to stand. Stand firm then, with the belt of truth buckled around your waist, with the breastplate of righteousness in place, and with your feet fitted with the readiness that comes from the gospel of peace. In addition to all this, take up the shield of faith, with which you can extinguish all the flaming arrows of the evil one. Take the helmet of salvation and the sword of the Spirit, which is the word of God. And pray in the Spirit on all occasions with all kinds of prayers and requests. With this in mind, be alert and always keep on praying for all the Lord's people" (Ephesians 6:10–18).

God gives us the belt of truth—the foundation that holds everything together. His Word is His truth, His very mind written out for us, giving us discernment to recognize what is true and what is a lie. When the enemy whispers, "You can't do it," "You'll fail," "You're not good enough," or "You won't make it," the belt of truth counters with God's promises: You are fearfully and wonderfully made. You are more than a conqueror through Christ. "My plans for you are to prosper you, not to harm you."

When I left home as a child at 15, I didn't fully understand God, but something deep inside refused to let the enemy's voice dictate my future. The truth I held on to was that staying would mean the death of my spirit, my mind, and my hope. I didn't know much about God, but I knew enough to have hope—a hope that there was something better, something safer ahead. The same truth sustained me when I loaded my sons, a few belongings, and even the dog into the car and fled my abusive marriage. The enemy whispered every reason I should stay: *You'll fail. You won't survive. You'll be worse off.* But the truth was clear: If I stayed, the outcome could be far worse. God was my hope then, just as He is now. The discernment God gives us—the ability to recognize His voice above all others—is a weapon. It allows us to identify the enemy's lies and stand firm in His truth. Whether it's fleeing a toxic environment or stepping into the unknown, God equips us with His armor and His promises, and through Him, we can overcome every obstacle. The enemy may try to plant seeds of doubt, fear, and hopelessness, but God's truth uproots those lies and reminds us that with Him, all things are possible.

The Breastplate of Righteousness

The enemy is a master manipulator, planting lies in your heart and mind to convince you that every negative word spoken over you is the truth. He tells you that you're unworthy, not good enough, a failure. He whispers that you're stupid, ugly, and incapable of being loved—not by others, and certainly not by God. But God, in His infinite wisdom and grace, has given us the Breastplate of Righteousness to guard our hearts against these lies. This breastplate is not our righteousness but God's. It is His declaration over us that we are worthy, valuable, and deeply loved—not because of what we've done but because of who He is. As I reflect on my journey, I remember the moment my spiritual mother gave me a word from God through Isaiah 43:1–8.

In it, one verse brought me to tears of gratitude and overwhelming emotion: "Since you were precious in My sight, You have been honored, And I have loved you" (Isaiah 43:4).

To know that God not only loves me but considers me precious in His sight—do you understand the magnitude of those words? As a girl who had never felt valuable to anyone, for God, the Creator of the universe, to declare this about me? It shook me to my core. I remember crying out,

"Who am I, Lord, that You would say such a thing? I have failed You so many times. I am no one." Yet God's response, through His Word, was firm and unwavering: "You are someone. You are precious. You are honored. You are loved."

Those words changed me. To know that I am precious to Him, that He loves me not because I earned it but because He chose to, filled a void in my heart that no one else could ever touch. The love of God is unlike any love we can experience in this world. It's pure, unwavering, and unconditional. Through the Breastplate of Righteousness, God says to us: "You are worthy. You are valuable. You are righteous—not because of who you are but because of who I am. Not because of what you've done but because of what I've done for you."

The enemy can no longer manipulate me into believing his lies because my heart is shielded by God's truth. When the voice of doubt tries to creep in, I remind myself of what God has declared: I am precious in His sight. I am loved by Him. He has plans for me, and He calls me righteous. God's love is transformative. It turns the broken into the whole, the unworthy into the honored, and the rejected into the chosen. Because He says so, I know I am someone, and that truth silences every lie the enemy tries to speak over me.

CHAPTER 6

Fitted Feet

Walking in Boldness and Strength

For much of my life, fear was a weapon used to silence me. It was a weapon that succeeded for far too long. I could list countless reasons for my silence: embarrassment, pride, lack of self-worth, and, most of all, the paralyzing fear of the consequences of speaking up. I feared judgment, criticism, rejection, disappointment, and, of course, the potential for more abuse. These fears kept me shackled and voiceless. But God didn't create us to walk in fear. He has fitted our feet with boldness and strength. He didn't design us for timidity or cowardice. When Jesus walked this earth, proclaiming the gospel and the promises of the Father, He did so with boldness and unwavering strength. He faced rejection, criticism, and opposition at every turn, yet He continued. If He had walked in fear or hesitation, would we have truly received the life-giving message of salvation? No!

His boldness ensured the Word reached us, untainted and powerful. It wasn't easy for me to find my voice. Fear constantly whispered, "No one will listen. No one cares to hear your testimony. You'll speak only to deaf ears." But I learned that God has given me fitted feet—feet prepared to stand firm and move forward, even when the ground beneath me feels shaky. These are feet strengthened by His Word, feet empowered to carry His message, feet that refuse to crumble under the weight of fear. I've learned to be a voice, even when fear told me to remain silent. I've learned to stand, even when my knees wanted to buckle. Why? Because I trust that God has called me to walk boldly. I trust that He has equipped me to speak out, to share my testimony, and to overcome the lies of the enemy. And now, I am writing this for you—every single one of you who feels voiceless, who believes that silence is your only option, who thinks you're too weak to stand against the lies and schemes of the enemy. I'm here to tell you this: God has given you fitted feet.

These feet are not made for retreating in fear or standing idly in uncertainty. They are made to carry you forward in strength and confidence. They are made to help you stand firm against the attacks of the enemy and to proclaim the truth boldly. So, take heart. Stand tall. Let the boldness God has fitted to your feet carry you where He has called you to go. Fear has no place in your walk. Trust Him, and you'll find that your feet are strong enough to carry you through any challenge, any trial, and any storm. You are not weak, you are not voiceless, and you are certainly not alone. God is with you, and He has equipped you to walk in His strength.

Shield of Faith: The Ultimate Defense Against Fear

Wow, did the weapon of fear work heavily on me through most of my life. I'm sure you've heard the phrase, "faith over fear"—it's on sweatshirts, coffee mugs, and everywhere you look these days. But let me tell you, it's not just a trendy saying; it's the truth. Faith and fear cannot coexist. One will always overpower the other. And guess which one the enemy loves to amplify? Fear. The enemy uses fear to discourage you, stifle you, and keep you stagnant in your situations. Fear will paralyze you, cloud your judgment, and lead you to make poor decisions that are outside of God's will for your life. I know this because I've lived it. One of the decisions that weighed heavily on my conscience for many years was the choice to terminate two pregnancies.

Let me be vulnerable here. In the late 1990s, when my sons were very young, my ex-husband was deeply entangled in drug use and abusive behaviors. I became pregnant—twice. Despite attempting to prevent it, I found myself in a situation that terrified me. I loved children, and I loved being a mother. But the thought of bringing another life into the chaos of my circumstances—struggling to provide, feeling broken, and living in an environment of drugs and violence—was too overwhelming. I let fear take over. Instead of turning to God, I relied on my limited understanding and chose what seemed like the only option: I ended those pregnancies. Even as I made that decision, my heart was heavy with grief and dread. Deep down, I knew it wasn't right. But I allowed fear to silence my faith, to override the trust I should have had in God.

Here's the irony: When I was pregnant with my sons, I was in a similar situation—barely getting by, surrounded by dysfunction. But God provided. He made a way for me and my children. Yet, in my fear, I forgot His faithfulness. I chose to take matters into my own hands, and it's a decision that changed me forever. Throughout the years, I've wondered if God was punishing me for those choices. I've thought about who my babies might have been, what they would have looked like, and the joy they could have brought to my life. But here's what I've learned: We serve a forgiving God. He doesn't condemn us for our mistakes; instead, He offers us grace, healing, and the chance to learn and grow. I share this not to judge or condemn but to remind you that fear is a liar.

It will push you into decisions that are not yours to make, decisions that rob you of peace and leave lasting wounds. God is the giver of life, and I allowed fear to convince me to step outside of His authority. I didn't trust Him, and that lack of trust led me down a path I now regret. So, what does it mean to have faith? It means trust. Trusting God even when the road ahead is dark and uncertain. Trusting Him when every negative voice inside you screams otherwise. Trusting Him when you feel the urge to take matters into your own hands. Faith isn't easy, but it's worth it. Faith gives you strength, clarity, and discernment. Faith silences the enemy's voice and fills you with confidence that, no matter the storm, God will lead you through it. Having faith means believing that God will not leave you in the pit. He will make a way out, a way through, and a way forward. He has promised us that we are more than conquerors. With the shield of faith, you can stand firm, extinguishing the flaming arrows of fear and doubt that the enemy throws your way. Faith is your power. Trust in it. Trust in Him.

The Helmet of Salvation: Your Divine Protection

The Helmet of Salvation is more than a symbol—it's a declaration and a shield. It represents "the deliverance, by the grace of God, from eternal punishment for sin that is granted to those who accept by faith God's conditions of repentance and faith in the Lord Jesus." This truth is profound and transformative. I remember the first time I stepped into a church and heard the teaching on salvation. It was the promise of God to not only deliver me from the punishment of sin but also to be my source of strength, my weapon against the enemy, and my continual fountain of grace and peace. Yet, throughout my journey, God had to continually remind me of who I was: a daughter of the Most High, righteous because of His grace and love for me. I carry His armor. I am more than a conqueror. I am saved, redeemed, transformed, delivered, and cherished by my Heavenly Father.

Salvation Is Active, Not Passive

Salvation is not just about reciting a prayer or standing at the pulpit in agreement with a pastor. It's about truly wearing the helmet and believing it was tailor-made for you. It's about understanding that this helmet is your divine protection, designed to provide all that God has promised. When you declare Jesus as your Savior, when you acknowledge that He died for your sins, and when you ask for forgiveness, inviting Him into your heart, mind, spirit, and life—you have to mean it. And meaning it requires action. You must actively wear that helmet every day.

Understanding the Commitment

When I first became saved, I thought I understood what it meant. I grasped the basic concept, but I didn't fully comprehend the depth of the commitment. Salvation isn't just a one-time decision; it's a daily surrender. Sometimes, it's even a moment-by-moment submission. Why? Because the devil is always waiting for an opening. Without that helmet securely in place, he'll slip into your mind, whispering lies: "You're not worthy." "You're not protected." "You're not redeemed." And without the helmet, it's easy to believe him.

Wearing the Helmet of Salvation

To truly wear the Helmet of Salvation means to continually seek God in every situation, every doubt, and every uncertainty. It means leaning into His truth when the world—and the enemy—tries to fill your mind with lies. It's about trusting in His promises, even when you don't fully understand them. Wearing the helmet is about protection and proclamation. It's saying, "I belong to God," and living that truth every day. It's allowing His grace to remind you of who you are: chosen, loved, and saved. It's a commitment to keep your mind and heart aligned with His, recognizing that salvation is not just a ticket to eternity but a source of strength, peace, and identity in the here and now.

CHAPTER 7

PRAYER

THE POWER TO SILENCE FEAR AND CONQUER THE ENEMY

Prayer is the weapon we wield to fight every attack, silence every negative voice, and shut down fear. As I grew in my spiritual journey, I began to understand that prayer is my direct line to God—my Heavenly Father, my source of strength, and my ultimate guide. Think about how you pick up the phone to call your best friend, dial a number to make a medical appointment, or press 911 in an emergency. God is all of that and more. Prayer is the call that connects you straight to His ears. He's waiting to hear from you, longing for that conversation. He wants you to turn to Him with your needs, desires, concerns, and even your fears.

The Power of Prayer

The Bible tells us: "Confess your faults one to another, and pray one for another, that ye may be healed. The effectual fervent prayer of a righteous man availeth much" (James 5:16). Prayer is powerful. It's where we experience the divine connection between us and our Heavenly Father. It's through prayer that the voice of God can be heard, where miracles are ignited, where healing begins, where deliverance takes place, and where breakthroughs are born.

God Invites You to Seek Him

God isn't distant or inaccessible. He wants you to seek Him, to spend time in His presence, and to rely on the authority He has given you. Prayer is more than just words; it's a lifeline, an intimate connection, and a declaration of trust. He has equipped us with power through prayer: "I have given you authority to trample on snakes and scorpions and to overcome all the power of the enemy; nothing will harm you" (Luke 10:19). God has given us the authority to conquer fear, overcome the enemy, and pull down every stronghold that seeks to bind us. Fear, doubt, and anxiety are silenced when we engage in fervent prayer, trusting in God's power to work in every situation.

The Call to Prayer

Prayer is an invitation to activate the power God has already placed within you. It's not just a ritual or a task—it's the very essence of your relationship with Him. When you pray, you're not just speaking words into the air; you're stepping into His presence, aligning yourself with His will, and declaring His promises over your life. So, pick up the phone, make that call, and pour your heart out to the One who loves you unconditionally. Use the authority He has given you to trample over fear, to stand firm against the enemy, and to claim the victory He has already won for you. Through prayer, you are more than a conqueror—you are a child of God, equipped and empowered to overcome.

Strongholds

Spiritual strongholds are deeply ingrained patterns of negative emotions and thoughts that obstruct our spiritual growth and weaken our relationship with God. These strongholds often find their footing in past traumas, current difficulties, and the fear of an uncertain future. Emotional strongholds, in particular, have many faces—self-esteem issues, anxiety, and fear being some of the most common.

The Connection Between Emotions and Thoughts

Our emotions are directly influenced by our thoughts, and those thoughts often stem from our circumstances. Imagine a cycle: Painful experiences lead to negative thoughts, which then feed unhealthy emotions, creating a stronghold that feels impossible to escape. In my journey, abuse played a significant role in forming such strongholds. My abuser's words and actions didn't just harm my body—they attacked my spirit. I was told, over and over, that I was worthless, that I deserved the abuse, and that I had no hope or future. At first, these were just words. But as they echoed in my mind, they took root, becoming the lens through which I viewed myself and my circumstances. The result? Fear consumed me. Worry became my constant companion. My emotions were battered as if they were being hit with a baseball bat, leaving me depleted and broken.

Recognizing the Stronghold

The first step in breaking free is recognizing that these patterns are not from God. The enemy uses lies, fear, and manipulation to build strongholds in our minds. He feeds us thoughts of inadequacy, hopelessness, and defeat to keep us bound. But here's the truth: You are not worthless. God created you in His image (Genesis 1:27). You are not deserving of abuse. God's plans for you are to prosper and not harm you (Jeremiah 29:11). You are not hopeless. Through Christ, you have hope and a future (Romans 15:13).

Breaking the Chains

Identify the Lie: What false beliefs are feeding your emotions? Confront them with the truth of God's Word.

Renew Your Mind: Meditate on scriptures that declare God's promises for your life.
Pray for Deliverance: Invite God into your pain and ask Him to help you dismantle the stronghold.

Speak Life: Replace negative self-talk with affirmations of God's truth.

God's Promise of Freedom

Remember, God does not intend for us to live in bondage. He has given us the tools—His Word, prayer, and the Holy Spirit—to tear down every stronghold. As 2 Corinthians 10:4–5 reminds us, "The weapons we fight with are not the weapons of the world. On the contrary, they have divine power to demolish strongholds." You are not defined by your trauma, your circumstances, or your past. You are defined by who God says you are: loved, redeemed, and chosen. Trust Him to heal your heart and restore your joy, for He is the ultimate chain breaker.

My strongholds were fear, worry, a lack of self-worth, and an addiction to the hope of finding love in someone who could give me what I was longing for: love without pain, security, provision, friendship, joy, and peace. After divorcing my ex-husband, I sought these things in other men, convincing myself that I could date and eventually find someone better suited for me. This mindset led me down a path of unhealthy relationships and behaviors that only brought me to a dead end. I was still trapped in a cycle of worthlessness and fear, wanting to feel wanted but doubting that I could ever measure up to what a good man would desire in a good woman. I told someone recently, "Until you work on yourself, identify who you are, and understand your worth, you won't have the eyes to recognize what is truly good—because all you've known is what isn't."

After countless failed attempts and encountering the same red flags I had endured in my marriage, I reached my breaking point. I was tired. Tired of repeating the same patterns, tired of the disappointment, and tired of looking for fulfillment in the wrong places. I finally made the decision to lay it down. I told myself, "I need to know who I am. I need to value myself, and I need God to give me a new lens to see life through." The problem was that I had been seeking everything I needed and wanted in a man, rather than focusing on God—the true source of all I was longing for. Don't get me wrong, I'm not saying love, companionship, and intimacy are bad. But the way I was seeking them was all wrong. I was relying on my own understanding, which had been shaped by trauma, deceit, and conditional love.

My way wasn't working because it was the only way I knew—one rooted in pain and brokenness. I needed to surrender: my way, my fear, my worry. I needed to let God take the driver's seat. And when we step out of God's way, He always provides exactly what we need, exactly when we need it. My biggest stronghold—one carefully molded by fear and anxiety—was the constant need to keep everything together. *I have to pay the bills, I have to keep working, I have to be a good wife, a good friend, a good mother. I have to plan the future. I have to, I have to, I have to.* These weren't just roles I knew I should fulfill; they became a never-ending cycle of worry and self-imposed pressure. This daily battle wasn't about doing my best; it was about worrying endlessly.

Worrying about whether I was doing enough, whether I was enough. The weight of this fear led to anger, frustration, and complete mental and physical exhaustion. I realized that, once again, I was allowing fear to rule over me. I had made fear my master. But here's the truth: We cannot serve two masters. We will either serve fear, anxiety, and self-reliance, or we will serve God. I had to make a choice—a decision that required full submission and surrender. It wasn't easy. I had to reach deep down into the bottom of my soul and pull out every pocket of fear and worry, every piece of control I was gripping tightly, and lay it at God's feet. Why? Because to truly see God's hand at work in my life, I had to stop smacking His hand away. Imagine someone offering to help you open a jar that's sealed so tight it feels impossible to budge. Yet, your pride says, "I can do it myself," so you smack their hand away, determined to handle it on your own. Isn't that what we often do with God? We exert our will, take control, and say, "I got this." But let's be real—do we really have it? I had to admit that I didn't. I had to look up and say, "God, please, by Your strength, not my own, open this jar!" And when I finally did, when I truly surrendered, I saw His power and His grace pour into every area of my life.

When I reflect on the origin of fear in humanity, I'm drawn to its first appearance in human emotion. It all began in the Garden of Eden, when Adam and Eve ate from the tree they had been explicitly instructed to avoid. In that moment, their eyes were opened, and they became aware of their nakedness. When they heard God walking in the Garden, they were afraid. Why? Because they had made the conscious choice to disobey His command. With that choice came a profound awareness of good and evil—a knowledge that carried the weight of shame and the sting of fear.

They were no longer innocent; they now understood the consequences of their actions and dreaded what God might say or do. Fear entered their hearts, born of guilt and the realization of their separation from Him. Let's take a broader view of fear—one that goes beyond our personal traumas or individual experiences. Fear is deeply woven into the fabric of a world filled with sinful acts. Yes, we see immeasurable violence, sexual violations, crime, and other atrocities. But fear doesn't just stem from those extreme acts—it's also fueled by the expectations society places on us. Society dictates how we should look, dress, speak, move—or even how we shouldn't. It decides what's acceptable or unacceptable, who fits into its carefully crafted norms, and who doesn't. Children are pressured to follow fleeting trends to avoid ridicule. Adults are pushed to embody society's definition of success, beauty, intelligence, or entertainment. These demands create an undercurrent of anxiety, depression, and oppression.

At the heart of it all is a fear: fear that we won't measure up, that we'll fail, that we won't be accepted. In striving to meet these ever-changing standards, we've taken our eyes off the One who defines our worth—God. We've traded His truth about who we are for the world's fleeting opinions. We've allowed the carnal demands of society to become our god. And the result? A world gripped by fear, with people walking around terrified of failure, rejection, and insignificance. The enemy doesn't even need to lift a finger; he simply sits back and enjoys the show, watching us crumble under the weight of these self-imposed idols. It's only when we remember where our true identity and success come from that we can break free from this fear and walk boldly in the freedom God intended for us.

What is idolatry? Simply put, it is the worship of other gods—anything or anyone we elevate above the one true God. But how does fear tie into this? The connection is clear: Fear often drives us to focus on, give time to, and make something or someone the center of our attention, even when it's the very thing that causes us pain. We worship people, we worship money, we worship material possessions, and we worship secular ideas and beliefs. Perhaps most subtly, we even worship our own trauma. How? By allowing it to dominate our thoughts, dictate our actions, and control both our present and our future. When trauma becomes the lens through which we view life, it becomes a god we serve—consuming our emotional, mental, physical, and spiritual energy.

When we idolize anything—be it people, possessions, beliefs, or pain—we take our eyes off God. We sacrifice our peace, joy, and trust in Him for the sake of something that ultimately cannot sustain or save us. Idolatry isn't just bowing to a statue; it's giving anything the power to rule over us and consume the place that belongs to God alone. True freedom begins when we shift our focus back to God, allowing Him to heal, guide, and lead us into the abundant life He intended.

When I reflect on my life and the moments I truly cried out to God—not with a shallow request, but with a desperate, wholehearted plea—He answered. When I had no food to feed my children, I called on God for provision, and He answered. When I sought deliverance from the bondage of abuse, He answered. When I was in the darkest depths of despair, seeking death as an escape from my pain, God commanded death to pass me by. When my rent was stolen, my car payment was taken, and my utilities were on the verge of being shut off, I cried out to Him, and He made a way out of no way. What I want you to understand is this: When you fully surrender whatever you are facing to God—when you let go of control with a sincere heart—He does answer. He does deliver. He does provide.

The greatest power God has given us is prayer. His Word declares that the fervent, effectual prayer of the righteous availeth much. Yet, so often, we fail to tap into the full power of prayer because we approach it with the wrong mindset. The Bible tells us to seek first the Kingdom of God and His righteousness, but instead, we often seek our own desires first. We receive not because we ask not. And even when we do ask, we sometimes do so with fleshly motives, selfish desires, or without a sincere heart. I prayed many times, but I also held tightly to the steering wheel of my life. So, were my prayers truly a cry for God's intervention? Or was I still trying to control the outcome? It was only when I fully submitted, when I released my grip and sincerely cried out to Him, that God responded. You see, prayer is more than just words we speak—it is an intimate connection, a heartfelt conversation, and a divine weapon placed in our hands by the Father. When we pray with faith, fully surrender, and trust in God, we activate a power that silences the enemy, binds the hands of his works, and positions us to receive victory from the Father.

Prayer is not just something we do—it is the key to unlocking God's presence, provision, and power in our lives. If we truly believe, if we truly surrender, we will see the hand of God move in ways beyond what we could ever imagine. God is sovereign. He moves as He wills, when He wills, and in the way He sees fit. Yet, in His sovereignty, there is grace, there is mercy, and there is a love so vast and immeasurable that it surpasses any love we could ever experience here on earth. In His sovereignty, God has given us a spirit of love, power, and a sound mind. He has not given us fear. He has not called us to doubt. He has not turned His back on us or declared that because we have free will, He will refuse to step in and help. No! His Word says: "Ask, and you shall receive." "Seek Me first, and all things will be added unto you." "Pray steadfastly, and I will hear your cries." "Abide in Me, and I will abide in you."

You see, yes—God has given us free will, but that does not mean He has abandoned us. Instead, He stands at the door of our hearts, waiting, asking: "Because you have the power to choose—will you choose Me? Will you ask Me? Will you trust Me?" God has not withheld Himself from us. He is ready. He is listening. The question is—will we surrender and seek Him first? Look back at my life—my testimony to you. Do you not see that I should have been dead? Do you not see that I should have lost my mind? Do you not understand that everything I've been through—and believe me, there is more than I could ever put into words—was not because God didn't answer my cries but because I cried out while still trying to control the outcome myself? God will not force Himself into your heart. He will not make you trust Him. Could He? Of course—He is God, and He can do all things. But if He did, it would make His gift of free will a lie. And God is not a man that He should lie.

What I have come to understand is that God was always there. He was waiting, listening, ready to move—but I had to choose Him. I had to let go. I had to surrender, fully and completely. And that's what He is waiting for from you. Listen: No matter what you have endured in life, God is not the cause. Yet, so often, we are quick to blame Him for everything, crying out, "Why, God? Why me? Why this?" But here's a hard question—why not you? Looking back on my life, I had to face a truth that changed everything: Did God delay my deliverance, my healing, my provision? Or did I delay God by trying to manage it my way? Was everything I went through meaningless suffering? Or was there purpose in it—to truly know God, to trust Him, and to be able to sit here now, writing these words to you? To tell you from firsthand experience that God does deliver, He does answer the call, and He does equip us with the weapons to silence the lies of fear. The truth is, God never fails—but we must let go of our need to control and truly surrender. That's when the breakthrough comes.

I've heard many people say—and I was once guilty of this myself—"I don't know how to pray. I don't know what to say to God." But seriously, stop overcomplicating it. He is God. He is the Creator of you. He already knows how you speak—whether with eloquence or simplicity. Do you really think He cares how you deliver your words to Him? Or does it matter more that you just come to Him, no matter how plain, raw, or unpolished your words may be? Do you not remember earlier in this book when I shared how, during my ex-husband's time in jail and my children's summer visit with their grandmother, I yelled at God? I cried, I screamed, I let out everything in my heart—no matter how messy or unrefined it sounded. And yet, God listened. God doesn't care about fancy words—He cares about your heart. He cares that you reach out to Him with sincerity, with an authentic cry, with a faith as small as a mustard seed that simply says: "God, I don't have all the answers.

I don't even know what to say. But one thing I do know is this—I can't do this without You." That's the prayer that moves mountains. That's the prayer God is waiting to hear. You see, fear was my captor—not my ex-husband, not my stepfather. Fear was the force that kept me bound. But when I sincerely went to God and asked Him to help me, He did not delay. Now, I won't tell you that it happened overnight. For some, deliverance comes in an instant; for others, it's a process. But hear me—there is a mighty purpose in the process. And I won't lie to you and say that fear—the enemy's weapon—will never try to creep back into your thoughts and emotions. It will. But what I can tell you is this: God has equipped me. He has clothed me in His armor. He has filled me with His glorious power. And because of that, I now have the authority to silence fear every time it tries to whisper in my ear. And so do you. Let me tell you this—drown yourself in His Word. Now, I don't mean stop going to work or neglect your responsibilities, but I do mean that you must seek Him not only in prayer but also in His Word. Because His Word is the only blueprint you will ever need to build your life.

One thing I know with absolute certainty is this: The Word of God is your weapon of truth. It is how He speaks to you. It is His foolproof instruction for how we are to live—and how we are not to live. When I pray, I hear God's Word echoing in my heart and spirit. He comforts me, educates me, nourishes me, and even disciplines me through His Word. God does not want us to be naïve to the enemy's tactics. He does not want us to be vulnerable, easily manipulated, or blindly led into destruction. The enemy has one mission: to kill, steal, and destroy—our minds, our bodies, and our spirits. But here's what you must understand: It's not even about you. The enemy's attacks on your life? The trials, the setbacks, the moments where you've questioned your worth? It was never really about you—it has always been about proving God wrong. Satan wants to prove that we are unworthy. That we will fail. That we will disappoint God. That his power over us will prevail.

Let's not forget why Lucifer was cast out of Heaven—pride, rebellion, and his desire to be greater than God. His war is not just with you; his war is against God Himself. And because God has chosen us, because we are precious in His sight, Lucifer will do everything in his power to: Deter us. Discourage us. Destroy us. Why? Because every soul lost to destruction is one less disciple. One less servant. One less chosen one. One less for God. But if you stay rooted in His Word, if you seek Him first—you will not be one less.

You will be one more—one more soul standing in victory, one more warrior equipped for battle, one more light that darkness cannot overcome.

The journey has not been easy. The road to righteousness is narrow, and it requires endurance, faith, and a constant battle against the whispers of fear. Fear must be silenced repeatedly, reminded that it has no authority, and commanded to return to the pit from which it came. But despite the struggles, this journey has transformed me. It has given me a life—a real life—one that, though still filled with challenges, is also filled with promise. It is a life covered by God's grace, secured by His love, and guided by His sovereign hand. "Suffer with Me now, and reign with Me later."

That is what God spoke to me one morning. And of course, the moment I heard it, here came that venomous snake—fear—trying to strike, trying to make me doubt, trying to shake my faith. But I have learned. I have grown. I now know how to pull the trigger on fear, to shut it down, and to command it to be silent in the name of Jesus! I refuse to bow to fear, because I belong to God. And in Him, victory is already mine. So, what will you do today? Will you continue to sit in your mess? Will you keep muttering empty words to God, asking for help while still pushing Him to the back seat, telling Him to wait because you got this? Will you ask God to help you, but then dictate to the All-Knowing, the All-Seeing exactly how you want Him to do it? Will you continue to be beaten up, beaten down, stolen from, lied to? Will you keep trying to fix the one who is hurting you, while making excuses for the hurt? Will you keep blaming God for the actions of sinful man? Will you keep choosing what you think is the right path, only to fall flat on your face in despair, anger, and loneliness? Or will you finally put on the armor of God, stand firm with your feet fitted for battle, and—even if all you have is a faith as small as a mustard seed—truly let God do what He does? God has already set out a plan for your life—a plan to prosper you, not to harm you.

A plan to give you hope and a future. God has already given you the power to tread on serpents and scorpions, the power to overcome every scheme of the enemy. God has not given you a spirit of fear. He has given you power. He has given you love. He has given you a sound mind. So, whatcha gonna do? Are you going to be like me—wasting years trapped in abuse, heartbreak, and stubbornness, delaying everything God had for me because I was afraid and hard-headed? NO! Stand up! Put your armor on! Cry out to God and mean it! Watch God work. He will—trust me; better yet, trust God! Fear not, and KNOW that He is God! I had to put my faith to work—not just say I believed, but live it, breathe it, and hold on to it even when I didn't feel it. Even when doubt whispered that I was alone. Even when the weight of my past threatened to crush me. I had to seek counseling.

I had to let go of my pride and allow myself to receive support from people who truly cared about me. I had to be transparent, peeling back the layers of pain and shame I had hidden behind for so long. I had to dive into God's Word, not just skimming the surface, but grasping His promises with everything in me—clinging to His faithfulness like my life depended on it. I had to ask God ... "Do You hear me?" I had to open my heart, open my mouth, and surrender, allowing God to take over. I had to stop white-knuckling the wheel of my life, trying to control every turn, every outcome. Even when I couldn't see the road ahead, I had to trust Him to drive. And let me tell you something—I cannot stress this enough—true submission and surrender to God is not passive. It is not weak. It is not easy. It is an all-consuming, gut-wrenching, tear-soaked cry that comes from the deepest part of your soul. You don't have to say it nicely. You don't have to phrase it perfectly. You just have to mean it. Tell God to help you. Tell Him to deliver you. Tell Him to save you. Does that sound dramatic? Well, so is your bondage to fear. Are you stuck? Are you drowning? Have you shut down so completely that you can't even envision the life you were meant to live? Then, yes, this is dramatic—and your cry to God should be even more dramatic. It should be raw.

Unfiltered. Transparent. And absolutely sincere. He will do it for you. But it has to start with you. I made the choice to give it to Him every single day—and sometimes every single minute. I prayed. I cried. I studied His Word. I sought out counsel. I let my loved ones see my brokenness instead of pretending I had it all together. And that process? That painful, humbling, terrifying process?

It forced me to open the door to my heart. And when I tell you that wasn't easy—I mean it. But it was worth it. I pushed through school. I focused on my mental, spiritual, and physical health. I raised my standards according to who God says I am—not what the world told me, not what my past told me, not what fear whispered to me in the dark. I let go of what needed to go—or rather, who needed to go. It wasn't easy. It didn't happen overnight. But it happened. And if it happened for me, it can happen for you, too.

Now, wait ... You're probably thinking, *Okay, Rose, you told us all about what you've been through, but what about where you are now?* Of course, the journey never truly ends—but let me tell you this: God brought me out. Out of bondage. Out of depression. Out of oppression. And yes—He has equipped me to shut down fear every time it tries to rise up. But that's not all. God has restored me. I now have a loving, supportive husband. I have two amazing sons, two wonderful stepchildren, and a whole handful of grandchildren who bring me so much joy. I have three college degrees. I work in mental health as a Human Resources Director for two companies. I have an awesome church family who loves me; I still have the love and support of my spiritual mother and family. But most importantly, God has given me a spirit of boldness to serve in ministry—as a prayer warrior for the body of Christ. And let me tell you—God is not done with me yet! As my Apostle, Bryan Andrew Wilson, once said, "It's a comma, not a period." I have peace in knowing that God is with me. I have love. I have boldness. And I have the full armor of God. This didn't happen overnight. But it happened. And if He did it for me, He can and WILL do it for you! Now, let me ask you: Have you received Jesus? Are you ready for Him?

If your answer is yes, then let's pray together:

Father,
Forgive me of my sins. I believe that Christ died on the cross for me, that through His sacrifice, I am redeemed and have received the promise of everlasting life. Today, I surrender—my mind, my body, and my spirit—to You. I ask You to come into my heart, into my life, and be my Savior. I open every door that was once locked to You and invite You in—as my God, my Father, my Strength, and my Savior. In the mighty, mighty name of Jesus, I pray.
Amen.

If you prayed this prayer with a sincere heart, know this—you are saved! You are now a child of God, covered by His grace, His mercy, and His unfailing love. Welcome to the family of Christ!

Now, let's—you and I, together—shut down the weapon of fear and silence the voice of the enemy. Pray with me:

Father God,
In the name of Jesus, we stand together in unity, authority, and faith, and we shut down the weapon of fear right now! Fear is not our portion, fear is not our future, and fear has no power over us! Your Word says that You have not given us a spirit of fear, but of power, love, and a sound mind (2 Timothy 1:7). So, right now, we rebuke the spirit of fear and command it to flee from our hearts, our minds, and our lives. Enemy, we silence your voice, your lies, your manipulations, and your distractions in Jesus' name! You will no longer torment us, steal our peace,

or plant doubt in our hearts. Every scheme, every trap, every deception you have set against us—we cancel it right now in the name of Jesus! We declare that God is our refuge and our fortress, that we are covered under the shadow of the Almighty (Psalm 91). We declare that no weapon formed against us shall prosper (Isaiah 54:17). We declare that we are victorious through Christ Jesus and that we will walk in boldness, authority, and faith, unshaken by fear! Lord, we thank You for filling us with Your presence, Your strength, and Your perfect peace. We thank You that fear has no dominion over us because we belong to You. In the mighty, mighty name of Jesus, we pray—AMEN!

IT. IS. DONE. Fear is silenced. The enemy is defeated. We stand in victory. Now walk boldly in your freedom!

Let's Pray Together:

Father God,
We come before You today with humble hearts and open spirits, asking You to fill us with boldness—the boldness that comes from knowing who we are in You. Right now, in the mighty name of Jesus, we cast down the spirit of timidity, self-doubt, and lack of self-worth. We rebuke every lie that has told us we are not enough, that we are unworthy, or that we are incapable. We reject the enemy's voice that tries to diminish us, and we stand on the truth of Your Word that says we are fearfully and wonderfully made (Psalm 139:14). Father, remind us of who You have called us to be. Remind us that we are precious in Your sight (Isaiah 43:4), that we are chosen, set apart, and called for a purpose (Jeremiah 29:11). You have not created us to shrink back in fear but to rise in faith, in courage, and in power! Lord, we ask You to

pour out a fresh anointing of confidence, strength, and boldness over our lives. Fill us with the fire of Your Spirit so that we walk in authority, knowing that we are Yours. Let every spirit of hesitation, insecurity, and fear fall powerless at Your feet. And in its place, let there be faith, courage, and unwavering trust in Your plan for us. We declare today that we are bold warriors, victorious in Christ, chosen by You, and equipped for every good work You have prepared for us. Thank You, Father, for reminding us who we are and whose we are. We receive Your strength, Your love, and Your confidence. In the mighty, powerful, undefeated name of Jesus, we pray—AMEN!

Walk in your boldness! You are called. You are chosen. You are precious in His sight!

A Prayer for Breaking the Chains of Addiction:

Heavenly Father,
I come before You today, standing in the gap for every soul bound by the chains of addiction. Lord, You are the Chain-Breaker, the Deliverer, and the Mighty Savior who sets captives free. I declare, in the mighty name of Jesus Christ, that every stronghold of addiction must bow before You! Father, I plead the blood of Jesus over every person caught in the grip of addiction—whether it be drugs, alcohol, pornography, gambling, lust, food, or any destructive habit that has taken hold of their life. I rebuke every demonic force that has set up camp in their minds, hearts, and bodies, and I bind the hands of the enemy that has sought to keep them in bondage! Satan, you have no power here! You have lied, deceived, and tormented God's people long enough. By the authority of Jesus Christ, I cancel your assignment! I tear

down every generational curse, every stronghold, every spirit of addiction that has enslaved God's children. You will no longer have dominion over their lives! Lord, I pray for supernatural healing. Reach deep into the broken places—the wounds, the pain, the traumas that led them into addiction in the first place. Heal their hearts, restore their minds, and renew their spirits. Let them find their identity not in their struggles, but in who You say they are—redeemed, loved, chosen, and set apart for Your glory! Father, give them strength to resist temptation. Fill them with Your Spirit so they will not be overcome by cravings, urges, or the enemy's whispers of defeat. Surround them with people who will speak life, hold them accountable, and encourage them in righteousness. Break the toxic relationships, sever the ungodly connections, and remove anything in their lives that keeps them bound to addiction. Lord, let freedom reign! Let Your power sweep through their lives like a rushing wind, burning away every chain that binds them. Let them taste and see that YOU are greater than any high, any bottle, any pleasure this world could ever offer. We declare victory! We declare freedom! We declare healing! In the mighty and matchless name of Jesus Christ, it is done!
Amen and Amen!

Breaking Free from the Addiction of Trying to Save Someone

I want to take a moment to talk to you about addiction—not just the addiction that enslaves a person, but the addiction that traps the ones who love them. My ex-husband was an addict. He still is to this day, bound by the grip of drugs and alcohol. For 20 years, I tried everything in my power to save him. I supported him, pushed him, ridiculed him, chastised him—anything I thought might make him wake up and want to stop. I fought battles with drug dealers. I worked double shifts to cover the bills he drained. I justified his behavior, blaming his addiction on past trauma. I lied for him. I defended him. I checked him into rehab after rehab, always finding reasons why he didn't stay: "The program was bad." "They allowed people to use drugs." "The neighborhood tempted him." "They didn't understand him." Blah. Blah. Blah. As I sit here writing this, I feel angry—not just at him, but at myself.

Angry at all the excuses I made. Angry at the truth I refused to see. The reality is, I wasn't helping him. I was enabling him. I became the devil's helper in keeping him bound because I made it easier for him to continue in his addiction. I remember a powerful moment in counseling when an associate pastor looked me in the eye and asked me: "Have you stopped asking God to change him and started asking God to change you?" I had spent years competing with this man's addiction, making his struggle the center of my world. And in the process, I lost myself. Here's the truth: You cannot make an addict change. You cannot love them enough to heal them. You cannot force them to be better. Only God can bring deliverance, and the addict has to want it for themselves. That's free will. What God did for me when I started praying for me was deliver me from my own bondage of addiction—because, simply put, I was addicted to trying to save him. But wake up and understand this: YOU ARE NOT GOD. Pray for your loved one, but submit them to God. Support them, but don't enable them. Love them, but don't love their addiction. And yes, that may mean you have to separate yourself until they decide to surrender. It may mean that you never go back. Either way, you must lay this person at the feet of the Lord and pray—not just for the addict, but for yourself. You have to trust God no matter the outcome. You have to realize that you need deliverance, too. You have to accept that you cannot be their savior. That is not your job. I lost myself for a long time trying to be the fixer. But the more I tried to control the outcome, the more I became part of the problem. Don't be the problem. Give the problem to GOD. And when you do, He will set YOU free, too.

A Letter to My Abusers

I FORGIVE YOU. Yes, you read that right. I forgive you. Not because what you did was excusable. Not because the pain you caused wasn't real. But because I refuse to be bound by it any longer. I pray that you ask the Father to forgive you. I pray that you surrender to Him completely, that you open your heart and your mind to the Savior who can cleanse you, redeem you, and make you whole. I pray that for those of you who are still among the living, you don't just seek forgiveness—but that you also find the strength to forgive yourself. Forgive those who hurt you. Forgive those who disappointed you. Forgive those who helped shape the brokenness inside of you—the same brokenness that led you to hurt me. I pray that before you take your last breath on this earth, you find life in Christ—and that the person you were, the person who caused harm, is put to death in Him. I pray that you receive not only forgiveness but also peace, redemption, and deliverance. I forgive you not only because my faith calls me to but because I choose to. You see, forgiveness is my freedom. I will not let fear, bitterness, or the enemy's schemes hold me hostage any longer. I will not allow what you did to me to keep me bound. I forgive because I want to live. I forgive because I refuse to carry the weight of your choices any longer. I forgive because I believe in the power of Christ—not just for me, but for you. I know what God has done in my life, how He has transformed me, healed me, and set me free. And I also know that He can do the same for you. I forgive you. And now, I walk forward without chains.

ABOUT THE AUTHOR

Rose Howard is a seasoned mental health professional with over 25 years of experience, as well as an entrepreneur, author, and passionate intercessor. She is an active member of Freedom of Atlanta Ministries, where her faith continues to flourish. Once held captive by trauma and fear, Rose now walks boldly in the freedom of God, using her story to inspire and empower women to embrace healing and live courageously. She is joyfully married to her best friend, Michael, and together they have built a beautifully blended family of four sons, two daughters, and nine cherished grandchildren. Rose is also a proud dog mom to three spoiled Bullies. Her mission is simple yet powerful: to help others close the door to fear and step confidently into their God-given boldness.

www.ingramcontent.com/pod-product-compliance
Lightning Source LLC
Chambersburg PA
CBHW061103100726
47911CB00012B/362

* 9 7 8 1 6 3 6 1 6 2 4 8 5 *